RELIGIONS
OF THE
WORLD

BUDDHISM

CHRISTIANITY

CONFUCIANISM

HINDUISM

ISLAM

JUDAISM

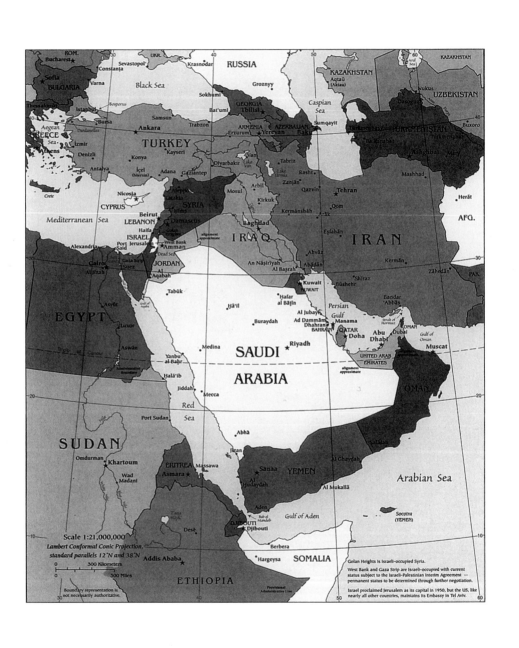

RELIGIONS
OF THE
WORLD

ISLAM

Masoud Kheirabadi
Professor of Islamic and Middle Eastern Issues
Portland State University

Series Consulting Editor **Ann Marie B. Bahr**
Professor of Religious Studies,
South Dakota State University

Foreword by **Martin E. Marty**
Professor Emeritus,
University of Chicago Divinity School

CHELSEA HOUSE
P U B L I S H E R S
A Haights Cross Communications Company
Philadelphia

FRONTIS This map of the Middle East shows Saudi Arabia, the country in which Islam originated, along with many of the nations where it has become the dominant faith.

CHELSEA HOUSE PUBLISHERS

VP, NEW PRODUCT DEVELOPMENT Sally Cheney
DIRECTOR OF PRODUCTION Kim Shinners
CREATIVE MANAGER Takeshi Takahashi
MANUFACTURING MANAGER Diann Grasse

Staff for ISLAM

EXECUTIVE EDITOR Lee Marcott
SENIOR EDITOR Tara Koellhoffer
PRODUCTION EDITOR Megan Emery
ASSISTANT PHOTO EDITOR Noelle Nardone
SERIES AND COVER DESIGNER Keith Trego
LAYOUT 21st Century Publishing and Communications, Inc.

A Haights Cross Communications ◀ Company

www.chelseahouse.com

First Printing

9 8 7 6 5 4 3 2 1

Library of Congress Cataloging-in-Publication Data

Kheirabadi, Masoud, 1951–
   Islam/by Masoud Kheirabadi.
      v. cm.—(Religions of the world)
Includes bibliographical references and index.
Contents: Muhammad—Qur'an—Worldview—Worship—Growing up
Muslim—Cultural expressions—Holidays—Memories—Islam in the
world today.
   ISBN 0-7910-7859-0 HC   0-7910-8012-9 PB
   1. Islam—Juvenile literature. [1. Islam.] I. Title. II. Series.
BP161.3.K48 2003
297—dc22
                                                    2003023919

11.95/7.17 Baker & taylor 3/05

CONTENTS

Foreword

On this very day, like all other days, hundreds of millions of people around the world will turn to religion for various purposes.

On the one hand, there are purposes that believers in any or all faiths, as well as unbelievers, might regard as positive and benign. People turn to religion or, better, to their own particular faith, for the experience of healing and to inspire acts of peacemaking. They want to make sense of a world that can all too easily overwhelm them because it so often seems to be meaningless and even absurd. Religion then provides them with beauty, inspires their souls, and impels them to engage in acts of justice and mercy.

To be informed citizens of our world, readers have good reason to learn about these features of religions that mean so much to so many. Those who study the faiths do not have to agree with any of them and could not agree with all of them, different as they are. But they need basic knowledge of religions to understand other people and to work out strategies for living with them.

On the other hand—and religions always have an "other hand"—believers in any of the faiths, and even unbelievers who are against all of them, will find their fellow humans turning to their religions for purposes that seem to contradict all those positive features. Just as religious people can heal and be healed, they can also kill or be killed in the name of faith. So it has been through history.

This killing can be literal: Most armed conflicts and much terrorism today are inspired by the stories, commands, and promises that come along with various faiths. People can and do read and act upon scriptures that can breed prejudice and that lead them to reject other beliefs and believers. Or the killing can be figurative, which means that faiths can be deadening to the spirit. In the name of faith, many people are repressed, oppressed, sometimes victimized and abused.

If religion can be dangerous and if it may then come with "Handle with Care" labels, people who care for their own security, who want to lessen tensions and inspire concord, have to equip themselves by learning something about the scriptures and stories of their own and other faiths. And if they simply want to take delight in human varieties and imaginings, they will find plenty to please them in lively and reliable accounts of faiths.

A glance at television or at newspapers and magazines on almost any day will reveal stories that display one or both sides of religion. However, these stories usually have to share space with so many competing accounts, for example, of sports and entertainment or business and science, that writers and broadcasters can rarely provide background while writing headlines. Without such background, it is hard to make informed judgments.

The series RELIGIONS OF THE WORLD is designed to provide not only background but also rich illustrative material about the foreground, presenting the many features of faiths that are close at hand. Whoever reads all six volumes will find that these religions have some elements in common. Overall, one can deduce that their followers take certain things with ultimate seriousness: human dignity, devotion to the sacred, the impulse to live a moral life. Yet few people are inspired by religions in general. They draw strength from what they hold particularly. These particulars of each faith are not always contradictory to those of others, but they are different in important ways. It is simply a fact that believers are informed and inspired by stories told in separate and special ways.

A picture might make all this vivid: Reading about a religion, visiting a place of worship, or coming into the company of those who believe in and belong to a particular faith, is like entering a room. Religions are, in a sense, spiritual "furnished apartments." Their adherents have placed certain pictures on the wall and moved in with their own kind of furnishings, having developed their special ways of receiving or blocking out light from such places. Some of their figurative apartments are airy, and some stress strength and security.

Philosopher George Santayana once wrote that, just as we do not speak language, we speak particular languages, so we have religion not as a whole but as religions "in particular." The power of each living and healthy religion, he added, consists in "its special and surprising message and in the bias which that revelation gives to life." Each creates "another world to live in."

The volumes in this series are introductions to several spiritual furnished apartments, guides to the special and surprising messages of these large and complex communities of faith, or religions. These are not presented as a set of items in a cafeteria line down which samplers walk, tasting this, rejecting that, and moving on. They are not bids for window-shoppers or shoppers of any sort, though it may be that a person without faith might be drawn to one or another expression of the religions here described. The real intention of the series is to educate.

Education could be dull and drab. Picture a boring professor standing in front of a class and droning on about distant realities. The authors in this series, however, were chosen because they can bring readers up close to faiths and, sometimes better, to people of faith; not to religion but to people who are religious in particular ways.

As one walks the streets of a great metropolis, it is not easy and may not even be possible to deduce what are the faith-commitments of those one passes unless they wear a particular costume, some garb or symbol prescribed by their faith. Therefore, while passing them by, it is not likely that one can learn much about the dreams and hopes, the fears and intentions, of those around them.

These books, in effect, stop the procession of passersby and bid visitors to enter those sanctuaries where communities worship. Each book could serve as a guide to worship. Several years ago, a book called *How to Be a Perfect Stranger* offered brief counsel on how to feel and to be at home among worshipers from other traditions. This series recognizes that we are not strangers to each other only in sanctuaries. We carry over our attachments to conflicting faiths where we go to work or vote or serve in the military or have fun. These "carryovers" tend to come from the basic stories and messages of the several faiths.

The publishers have taken great pains to assign their work to authors of a particular sort. Had these been anti-religious or anti–the religion about which they write, they would have done a disservice. They would, in effect, have been blocking the figurative doors to the faiths or smashing the furniture in the sanctuaries. On the other hand, it would be wearying and distorting had the assignment gone to public relations agents, advertisers who felt called to claim "We're Number One!" concerning the faith about which they write.

Fair-mindedness and accuracy are the two main marks of these authors. In rather short compass, they reach a wide range of subjects, focusing on everything one needs to advance basic understanding. Their books are like mini-encyclopedias, full of information. They introduce the holidays that draw some neighbors to be absent from work or school for a day or a season. They include galleries of notable figures in each faith-community.

Since most religions in the course of history develop different ways in the many diverse places where they thrive, or because they attract intelligent, strong-willed leaders and writers, they come up with different emphases. They divide and split off into numberless smaller groups: Protestant and Catholic and Orthodox Christians, Shiite and Sunni Muslims, Orthodox and Reform Jews, and many kinds of Buddhists and Hindus. The writers in this series do justice to these variations, providing a kind of map without which one will get lost in the effort to understand.

Some years ago, a rabbi friend, Samuel Sandmel, wrote a book about his faith called *The Enjoyment of Scriptures.* What an astonishing concept, some might think: After all, religious scriptures deal with desperately urgent, life-and-death-and-eternity issues. They have to be grim and those who read them likewise. Not so. Sandmel knew what the authors of this series also know and impart: that the journeys of faith and the encounter with the religions of others include pleasing and challenging surprises. I picture many a reader coming across something on these pages that at first looks obscure or forbidding, but then, after a slightly longer look, makes sense and inspires an "aha!" There are many occasions for "aha-ing!" in these books. One can also wager that many a reader will come away from the encounters thinking, "I never knew that!" or "I never thought of that before." And they will be more ready than they had been to meet strangers of other faiths in a world that so many faiths *have* to share, or that they *get* to share.

Martin E. Marty
The University of Chicago

Preface

The majority of people, both in the United States and around the world, consider religion to be an important part of their lives. Beyond its significance in individual lives, religion also plays an important role in war and peace, politics, social policy, ethics, and cultural expression. Yet few people feel well-prepared to carry on a conversation about religion with friends, colleagues, or their congressional delegation. The amount of knowledge people have about their own faith varies, but very few can lay claim to a solid understanding of a religion other than their own. As the world is drawn closer together by modern communications, and the religions of the world jostle each other in religiously plural societies, the lack of our ability to dialogue about this aspect of our lives results in intercultural conflict rather than cooperation. It means that individuals of different religious persuasions will either fight about their faiths or avoid the topic of religion altogether. Neither of these responses aids in the building of healthy, religiously plural societies. This gap in our knowledge is therefore significant, and grows increasingly more significant as religion plays a larger role in national and international politics.

The authors and editors of this series are dedicated to the task of helping to prepare present and future decision-makers to deal with religious pluralism in a healthy way. The objective scholarship found in these volumes will blunt the persuasive power of popular misinformation. The time is short, however. Even now, nations are dividing along religious lines, and "neutral" states as well as partisan religious organizations are precariously, if not always intentionally, tipping delicate balances of power in favor of one religious group or another with doles of aid and support for certain policies or political leaders. Intervention in the affairs of other nations is always a risky business, but doing it without understanding of the religious sensitivities of the populace dramatically increases the chances that even well-intentioned intervention will be perceived as political coercion or cultural invasion. With such signs of ignorance already manifest, the day of reckoning for educational policies that ignore the study of the world's religions cannot be far off.

This series is designed to bring religious studies scholarship to the leaders of today and tomorrow. It aims to answer the questions that students, educators, policymakers, parents, and citizens might have about the new religious milieu in which we find ourselves. For example, a person hearing about a religion that is foreign to him or her might want answers to questions like these:

- How many people believe in this religion? What is its geographic distribution? When, where, and how did it originate?

- What are its beliefs and teachings? How do believers worship or otherwise practice their faith?

- What are the primary means of social reinforcement? How do believers educate their youth? What are their most important communal celebrations?

- What are the cultural expressions of this religion? Has it inspired certain styles of art, architecture, literature, or music? Conversely, does it avoid art, literature, or music for religious reasons? Is it associated with elements of popular culture?

- How do the people who belong to this religion remember the past? What have been the most significant moments in their history?

- What are the most salient features of this religion today? What is likely to be its future?

We have attempted to provide as broad coverage as possible of the various religious forces currently shaping the planet. Judaism, Christianity, Islam, Hinduism, Buddhism, Confucianism, Taoism, Sikhism, and Shinto have each been allocated an entire volume. In recognition of the fact that many smaller ancient and new traditions also exercise global influence, we present coverage of some of these in two additional volumes titled "Tribal Religions" and "New Religions." Each volume in the series discusses demographics and geography, founder or foundational period, scriptures, worldview, worship or practice, growing up in the religion, cultural expressions, calendar and holidays, history, and the religion in the world today.

The books in this series are written by scholars. Their approach to their subject matter is neutral and objective. They are not trying to convert readers to the religion they are describing. Most scholars, however, value the religion they have chosen to study, so you can expect the general tone of these books to be appreciative rather than critical.

Religious studies scholars are experts in their field, but they are not critics in the same sense in which one might be an art, film, or literary critic. Religious studies scholars feel obligated to describe a tradition faithfully and accurately, and to interpret it in a way that will allow nonbelievers as well as believers to grasp its essential structure, but they do not feel compelled to pass judgment on it. Their goal is to increase knowledge and understanding.

Academic writing has a reputation for being dry and uninspiring. If so, religious studies scholarship is an exception. Scholars of religion have the happy task of describing the words and deeds of some of the world's most amazing people: founders, prophets, sages, saints, martyrs, and bodhisattvas.

The power of religion moves us. Today, as in centuries past, people thrill to the ethical vision of Confucianism, or the dancing beauty of Hinduism's images of the divine. They are challenged by the one, holy God of the Jews, and comforted by the saving promise of Christianity. They are inspired by the stark purity of

Islam, by the resilience of tribal religions, by the energy and innovation of the new religions. The religions have retained such a strong hold on so many people's lives over such a long period of time largely because they are unforgettable.

Religious ideas, institutions, and professions are among the oldest in humanity's history. They have outlasted the world's great empires. Their authority and influence have endured far beyond that of Earth's greatest philosophers, military leaders, social engineers, or politicians. It is this that makes them so attractive to those who seek power and influence, whether such people intend to use their power and influence for good or evil. Unfortunately, in the hands of the wrong person, religious ideas might as easily be responsible for the destruction of the world as for its salvation. All that stands between us and that outcome is the knowledge of the general populace. In this as in any other field, people must be able to critically assess what they are being told.

The authors and editors of this series hope that all who seek to wield the tremendous powers of religion will do so with unselfish and noble intent. Knowing how unlikely it is that that will always be the case, we seek to provide the basic knowledge necessary to critically assess the degree to which contemporary religious claims are congruent with the history, scriptures, and genius of the traditions they are supposed to represent.

Ann Marie B. Bahr
South Dakota State University

Author's Note

The tragic events of September 11, 2001, created a significant amount of interest in Islam and Muslims. Many concerned people throughout the world suddenly wanted to know if violence is an inherent part of Islam. Scholars and members of the media raise the question of "fundamentalism"; talk-show hosts discuss the connections between Islam and violence. Some sensationalist and controversy-seeking members of the media are attracted to Muslim radicals and extremists and often present these groups as the true representatives of Islam. This irresponsible journalism has smeared the image of Islam, especially in the United States, and has led to further misunderstanding of Islam and Muslims.

My main purpose for writing this book, however, is to introduce the authentic Islam to seeking minds. It can be essential reading for those with little or no knowledge of Islam; it can also enhance the knowledge and entice the curiosity of more advanced students of Islam and other religions. Readers will become familiar with the foundations of the religion and its similarities and differences with other monotheistic religions. Islam is studied as a way of life that affects all aspects of Muslim living, including the relationship with God, education, family dynamics, societal rules, art, entertainment, politics, technology, science, and civilization. The main focus of this book, however, remains the study of Islam as a spiritual path and its influence on an individual's spiritual growth.

In order to keep the study authentic, I have relied mainly on the Qur'an and ahadith (the prophet Muhammad's sayings) as my main sources of information. I have used a variety of the Qur'an's translations (Yusufali, Dawood, Pickthall, and Ahmad Ali,) and whenever necessary I have used my own judgment in interpretation of the words. For ahadith, I have relied mainly on al-Bukhari and Muslim as my major sources, though I have also utilized the wealth of information about the ahadith that can be found through helpful Internet Websites. For transliteration of Arabic terms, I have used those with the most accurate spellings.

Today, we live in pluralistic societies in an interdependent world. Our education should be based on facts rather than sensationalism. Accurate information about diverse cultures leads to better and more knowledgeable intercultural communication. Intercultural communication based on mutual understanding will make this world a better and much more peaceful place for all of us. My hope is that this book will serve as a small step toward that ideal goal.

August 21, 2003
Portland, Oregon

1

Introduction

By the bright morn, And by the night when all is still,
Thy Lord has not left thee, nor come to dislike thee. So the
latter situation will be better for thee than the former,
And thy Lord anon will assuredly give to thee that which
thou desirest, so that thou wilt be well content.

—The Qur'an 93:1–5

MEANING OF ISLAM

The term *Islam* is an Arabic word derived from the word *Salamah*, which means "peace." *Salamah* (or *salam*) shares similar roots with *shalom*, the Hebrew word that also means "peace." Since Arabic and Hebrew are sister languages that belong to the same Semitic language family, they share a similar vocabulary.

Another meaning of the word *Islam* is "submission" or "surrender." This refers to submission to the will of God. Muslims believe that submitting to the will of God and putting oneself in God's hands will lead to ultimate peace, which is considered the greatest accomplishment for humanity in the personal as well as societal domains.

Islam in another sense means "inner peace," a real peace for body and mind that is achieved through surrender and obedience to God. Here, surrender or submission to God out of love rather than fear is considered a positive act. It is an act of appreciation for all the benevolence that God has bestowed upon humanity; therefore, the word *submission* does not bear negative connotations as it often does in popular contexts.

ISLAM, NOT "IZLAM"

Many English-speaking people often mispronounce the word *Islam* as "Izlam," with a "Z" sound rather than an "S" sound. This mispronunciation can be considered very disrespectful to Muslims, since the wrong pronunciation could actually change the meaning of the word. To pronounce the word *Islam* correctly, one needs to pronounce the "I" sound short as in "itch", the "s" as in "sit", and the "a" as in "father" with the accent upon the last syllable, "-lam". Similar rules need to be followed when pronouncing the word *Muslim*. *Muslim* means "one who submits to God" and is used to describe an adherent of Islam. Islam (like Christianity) is the name of a religion, whereas a Muslim (like a Christian) is a follower of the religion of Islam. To pronounce the word *Muslim* correctly, one needs to pronounce the "u" sound as in "put", and "s" as in "sit", with the accent upon the first syllable, "Mus-". The word *Muslim* may also be spelled "Moslem;" however, the majority of Muslims prefer the use of "u" instead of "o" when spelling the term, and so "Muslim" is the form used here.

A MONOTHEISTIC RELIGION

The God of Islam is the same God who is worshiped by Christians and Jews. This deity is called *Allah* in Arabic and *Khoda* in Persian. However, the term *Allah*, which has been used frequently in the sacred scripture of Islam, the Qur'an (Koran), is the preferable name for God in Islam.

God (Allah), as mentioned in Qur'an, is the "Most Merciful," "the Most Compassionate." According to Muslims, God is the source of all existence. God is the creator and sustainer of the universe and all that it encompasses. In Islam, everything comes from God and everything eventually returns to God. God is beyond duality, trinity, or any other kinds of partnership. God has no body, no form, no gender, and no physical attributes. To Muslims, God is the ultimate reality, and belief in the existence of God is the first article of faith in Islam. The concept of God's oneness and the monotheism of Islam is called *Tawhid*. Tawhid is the cornerstone of the Islamic theological belief system. The following passage from the Qur'an will emphasize the concept of monotheism in Islam:

> In the Name of God, the Compassionate, the Merciful. God is One, the Eternal God. He begot none, nor was He begotten. None is equal to Him (Q. 112:1–4).

AN ETERNAL RELIGION

Unlike the term *Christianity*, which takes its name from the person of Jesus Christ, or *Judaism*, which is the religion of Jews, who originated from the tribe of Judah, the term *Islam* is not related to any particular person or group. Although the historical origins of Islam may be found in the seventh century A.D., according to Muslims, Islam has always been the natural religion of humankind. Throughout human history, all those who have consciously submitted to the will of God are considered Muslims. Muslims believe that Adam and Eve were the first people to submit to the will of God, and therefore, they were Muslims. According to Muslims, from the descendants of Adam and Eve came the prophet Noah (pronounced *Nooh* in Arabic), who had a son named Shem (*Saam* in Arabic). The word *Semitic* (or *Saami* in Arabic) is derived from *Shem*.

Abraham (called *Ibrahim* in Arabic) was a descendant of Shem, and he was married to a woman named Sarah. Because Sarah could not have a son, at her insistence, Abraham took a second wife, an Egyptian maid named Hagar (*Haajar* in Arabic). Hagar bore Abraham a son, who was named Ishmael (*Ismaaeel* in Arabic).

Later, by God's command, Sarah conceived and had a son, who was named Isaac (*Ishaaq* in Arabic). When Sarah had her own son, she demanded that Abraham banish Ishmael and Hagar from the tribe and send them somewhere remote so she would not have to see them anymore. With Ishmael and Hagar away, Sarah thought, Abraham would focus all his attention upon the newborn Isaac. As indicated in the Qur'an, God ordered Abraham to take Ishmael and Hagar to leave them somewhere in the Arabian Peninsula, at a place where the city of Mecca (*Makkah* in Arabic) was later founded.

Again by God's decree, Ishmael and his mother survived in the harsh desert and later reunited with Abraham. The descendants of Ishmael flourished in Arabia and became the Arabs. Thus, Ishmael was the forefather of the Arab people, and from his generation appeared the prophet Muhammad, who, according to Muslims, is the last of all the prophets.

The descendants of Isaac, on the other hand, remained in Palestine and flourished as the Hebrews, who were later called the Jews. From Isaac descended a number of prophets, including his son Jacob, his grandson Joseph, and others, such as Moses, John the Baptist, and Jesus. While Jews and Christians trace their history all the way back to Isaac, the son of Abraham and Sarah, Muslims trace their roots to Ishmael, the son of Abraham and Hagar, the Egyptian servant. Abraham is therefore considered the forefather of all monotheistic people—Jews, Christians, and Muslims. According to the Qur'an, Moses, David, and Jesus were all given scriptures by God. This means that they are all prophets of Islam. Islam recognizes all the prophets mentioned in the Bible as prophets of Islam and does not distinguish between them. The following verse in the Qur'an clarifies this concept:

> Say, O Muslims, we believe in Allah and in that which was revealed unto us and that which was revealed unto Abraham and Ishmael and Isaac and Jacob and the tribes, and that which Moses and Jesus received, and that which the Prophet received from the Lord. We make no distinction between any of them and unto Him we have surrendered (Q. 2:136).

A UNIVERSALIZING RELIGION

Like Christianity and Buddhism, Islam is a universal religion, meaning that the message of Islam is for the whole of humanity, no matter where they live in the world. This is in contrast with some religions, such as Judaism and Hinduism, which are considered "ethnic" religions—that is, their message is not intended for the whole of humanity but rather for a particular people who are usually concentrated in a certain geographic place in the world. Unlike Jews and Hindus, who do not actively seek converts, Muslims, like Christians, proselytize to spread their religion throughout the world. Like Christians and Buddhists, Muslim missionaries may be found in many different parts of the globe. Every Muslim is encouraged to spread the word of God and to call others to embrace the religion of Islam.

Due to its strict monotheistic approach to God, Islam is considered an exclusive religion. Unlike, for example, a Buddhist, who could be an adherent and practitioner of several religions at the same time, a Muslim cannot practice more than one religion at a time. In China, a person can be Buddhist, Confucian, and Taoist at the same time, but a Muslim *cannot* be a Buddhist. There are certain concepts unique to each religion that conflict with one another.

Because Islam believes that the way to salvation can be found only through monotheism, it accepts other monotheistic religions, such as Christianity and Judaism, as valid religions for humanity. In Islam, Christians and Jews are called "Peoples of the Book" because they follow prophets who were recipients of holy scriptures from God. Just as Muhammad received the Qur'an, Moses and Jesus received the Torah and the Gospel respectively, so they are also regarded as messengers of God by Muslims. (While Jews generally believe Moses was the actual author of the Torah, the Gospels contain the messages of Jesus as recorded by his followers in the decades after his death.) On the other hand, many Muslims view religions such as Hinduism and Buddhism as polytheistic (worshiping more than one god) in their approach to spirituality, and as a result, Muslims do not consider these authentic religions that will lead their followers to ultimate salvation.

A BOOK-BASED RELIGION

Historically speaking, Islam is the youngest of the world's monotheistic religions. Muhammad, the Prophet of Islam, was born 570 years after the birth of Jesus, in the city of Mecca in the Arabian Peninsula, the region known today as Saudi Arabia. Although Muhammad is considered the ideal man and the perfect role model for Muslims to emulate, he does not hold the same role in Islam that Jesus holds in Christianity. In Islam, it is the Qur'an—the sacred word of God revealed to Muhammad—and not Muhammad himself, that plays the central role. Thus, calling the religion of Islam "Muhammadanism" after Muhammad (as Christianity is named after Christ) as some Western writers have done erroneously assigns to Muhammad, rather than the Qur'an, the major function of Islam, a concept that would be considered blasphemous by many Muslims. Whereas in Christianity, the person of Jesus Christ is dominant, in Islam, God's words, the Qur'an, are the focus.

Recitation of the Qur'an as the precise words of God is considered an act of worship and remembrance of God by Muslims. Due to the strong emphasis on the Qur'an as the best gift possible from God as a guide for humanity, this scripture plays a fundamental part in Islam. The Qur'an consists of 114 *surah*, or chapters, that are unequal in length. Each chapter is divided into "verses" (although the Qur'an is not poetry) of varying numbers and lengths; each verse is called an *ayah*, or sign.

A RELIGION FOR ALL RACES

Islam originated in the Arabian Peninsula and from there spread to the rest of the world. However, today, Islam is not considered an exclusively Arab religion. Although the majority of Arabs are Muslims, the majority of Muslims are not Arabs. As a matter of fact, fewer than 20 percent of the world's Muslims are Arabs. The term *Muslim* does not carry any racial or ethnic connotations. Muslims can be Arab, Persian, Turk, German, French, American, or any other nationality.

Like Christians, Muslims are found all over the world, including Asia, Africa, Europe, Australia, and North and South America. Today there are more than fifty countries with a Muslim population majority. There are also millions of Muslims who live as significant minorities in other parts of the world. The most populous Muslim countries are actually located outside of the Arabian Peninsula where Islam originated. Among them are Indonesia, Bangladesh,

Pakistan, Iran, and Turkey. Egypt is the largest Arab Muslim country.

As the Qur'an shows, Islam rejects any concept of racism, sexism, nobility based upon descent, or hierarchy based upon social or economic class. Everybody is equal in the sight of God, and it is the degree of a person's righteousness and right conduct with which God is concerned:

> O humankind, We have created you male and female, and formed you into nations and tribes that you may recognize each other. However, the noblest of you in the sight of God is the best in conduct. God is all knowing and well informed (Q. 49:13).

POPULATION AND DISTRIBUTION OF MUSLIMS

The signs of Islam are seen all over the globe. There was once a time that a person had to travel to the Middle East to see mosques, minarets, and other symbols of Islam, but Muslims can now be found in most major cities throughout the world. In the United States, as in European countries where Muslims are minorities, Muslims are our neighbors and colleagues. They may dress in traditional or contemporary Islamic attire. Muslims also dress in everyday attire that makes them unrecognizable from non-Muslims. Like followers of Christianity, their approach to religion varies from very liberal to very conservative. Like many Christians who do not adhere strictly to principles of Christianity, many people who call themselves Muslims do not strictly follow the tenets of Islam.

Though the majority of Muslims are moderate in temperament and are very accepting of other religions, there are radical Muslims who are very exclusive in their approach to religion and who have no tolerance for acceptance of non-Muslims or even Muslims who do not think as they do. Unfortunately, these are the Muslims who often capture the attention of the Western media, and their behavior has resulted in a considerable amount of misunderstanding in the West about Islam and Muslims. Some

(Continued on page 13)

This Report Includes All The Countries Of The World And Shows How Many Muslims Are In Each One

Country Name	Total Population	Muslims %	Number of Muslims
Afghanistan	22,664,136	100	22,664,136
Albania	3,249,136	75	2,436,852
Algeria	29,183,032	99	28,891,202
Angola	10,342,899	25	2,585,725
Antigua and Barbuda	65,647	n/a	
Argentina	34,672,997	2	693,460
Aruba	67,794	5	3,390
Australia	18,260,863	2.09	382,000
Azerbaijan	7,676,953	93.4	7,170,274
Bahrain	590,042	100	590,042
Benin	5,709,529	15	856,429
Bangladesh	123,062,800	85	104,603,380
Bhutan	1,822,625	5	91,131
Bosnia and Herzegovina	2,656,240	40	1,062,496
Botswana	1,477,630	5	73,882
Brazil	162,661,214	0.6	1,000,000
Brunei	299,939	63	188,962
Bulgaria	8,612,757	14	1,205,786
Burkina Faso	10,623,323	50	5,311,662
Burma	45,975,625	10	4,597,563
Burundi	5,943,057	20	1,188,611
Cambodia	10,861,218	1	108,612
Cameroon	14,261,557	55	7,843,856
Canada	28,820,671	1.48	400,000
Central African Republic	3,274,426	55	1,800,934
Chad	6,976,845	85	5,930,318
China	1,210,004,956	11	133,100,545
Christmas Island	813	10	81
Cocos (Keeling) Island	609	57	347
Comoros	569,237	86	489,544
Congo	2,527,841	15	379,176
Cote d'Ivoire	14,762,445	60	8,857,467

Muslims are found in literally every country of the world, and their numbers are increasing. Although the Middle East and Asia, where Islam originated, still have the largest Muslim populations,

Country Name	Total Population	Muslims %	Number of Muslims
Croatia	5,004,112	1.2	60,049
Cyprus	744,609	33	245,721
Djibouti	427,642	94	401,983
Egypt	63,575,107	94	59,760,601
Equatorial Guinea	431,282	25	107,821
Eritrea	3,427,883	80	2,742,306
Ethiopia	57,171,662	65	37,161,580
Fiji	782,381	11	86,062
France	58,317,450	7	4,082,222
Gabon	1,172,798	1	11,728
Gambia	1,204,984	90	1,084,486
Gaza Strip	923,940	98.7	911,929
Georgia	5,219,810	11	574,179
Germany	83,536,115	3.4	2,840,228
Ghana	17,698,271	30	5,309,481
Gibraltar	28,765	8	2,301
Greece	10,538,594	1.5	158,079
Guinea	7,411,981	95	7,041,382
Guinea-Bissau	1,151,330	70	805,931
Guyana	712,091	15	106,814
Hong Kong	6,305,413	1	63,054
India	952,107,694	14	133,295,077
Indonesia	206,611,600	95	196,281,020
Iran	66,094,264	99	65,433,321
Iraq	21,422,292	97	20,779,623
Israel	5,421,995	14	759,079
Italy	57,460,274	1	574,603
Japan	125,449,703	1	1,254,497
Jordan	4,212,152	95	4,001,544
Kazakstan	16,916,463	51.2	8,661,229
Kenya	28,176,686	29.5	8,312,122
Kuwait	1,950,047	89	1,735,542
Kyrgyzstan	4,529,648	76.1	3,447,062
Lebanon	3,776,317	70	2,643,422
Liberia	2,109,789	30	632,937
Libya	5,445,436	100	5,445,436

as this chart demonstrates, many other nations have substantial numbers of Muslim residents. (Original chart is available online at: *http://www.geocities.com/zubairkhan_99/population.html*.)

Country Name	Total Population	Muslims %	Number of Muslims
Lesotho	1,970,781	10	197,078
Macedonia	2,104,035	30	631,211
Madagascar	13,670,507	20	2,734,101
Malawi	9,452,844	35	3,308,495
Malaysia	19,962,893	52	10,380,704
Maldives	270,758	100	270,758
Mali	9,653,261	90	8,687,935
Malta	375,576	14	52,581
Mauritania	2,336,048	100	2,336,048
Mauritius	1,140,256	19.5	222,350
Mayotte	100,838	99	99,830
Mongolia	2,496,617	4	99,865
Morocco	29,779,156	98.7	29,392,027
Mozambique	17,877,927	29	5,184,599
Namibia	1,677,243	5	83,862
Nepal	22,094,033	4	883,761
Netherlands	15,568,034	3	467,041
Niger	9,113,001	91	8,292,831
Nigeria	103,912,489	75	77,934,367
Norway	4,438,547	1.5	66,578
Oman	2,186,548	100	2,186,548
Pakistan	129,275,660	97	125,397,390
Panama	2,655,094	4	106,204
Philippines	74,480,848	14	10,427,319
Qatar	547,761	100	547,761
Reunion	679,198	20	135,840
Romania	21,657,162	20	4,331,432
Russia	148,178,487	18	26,672,127
Rwanda	6,853,359	1	68,534
Saudi Arabia	19,409,058	100	19,409,058
Senegal	9,092,749	95	8,638,112
Serbia and Montenegro	10,614,558	19	2,016,766
Sierra Leone	4,793,121	65	3,115,529
Singapore	3,396,924	17	577,477
Slovenia	1,951,443	1	19,514
Somalia	9,639,151	100	9,639,151

Country Name	Total Population	Muslims %	Number of Muslims
South Africa	41,743,459	2	834,869
Sri Lanka	18,553,074	9	1,669,777
Sudan	31,547,543	85	26,815,412
Suriname	436,418	25	109,105
Swaziland	998,730	10	99,873
Sweden	9,800,000	3.6	320,000
Syria	15,608,648	90	14,047,783
Tajikistan	5,916,373	85	5,028,917
Tanzania	29,058,470	65	18,888,006
Thailand	58,851,357	14	8,239,190
Togo	4,570,530	55	2,513,792
Trinidad and Tobago	1,272,385	12	152,686
Tunisia	9,019,687	98	8,839,293
Turkey	62,484,478	99.8	62,359,509
Turkmenistan	4,149,283	87	3,609,876
Uganda	20,158,176	36	7,256,943
United Arab Emirates	3,057,337	96	2,935,044
United Kingdom	58,489,975	2.7	1,579,229
United States	266,476,278	3.75	9,992,860
Uzbekistan	23,418,381	88	20,608,175
West Bank	1,427,741	75	1,070,806
Western Sahara	222,631	100	222,631
Yemen	13,483,178	99	13,348,346
Zaire	46,498,539	10	4,649,854
Zambia	9,159,072	15	1,373,861
Zimbabwe	11,271,314	15	1,690,697

media professionals who seek controversy have misrepresented extremist Muslims and their organizations as representative of Islam in general. Such an approach has distorted Western views of the religion of Islam.

Because not all Muslims visit Islamic mosques or other Islamic centers on a regular basis, estimating mosque memberships does not yield accurate statistical information about the number of

Muslims who reside in different countries, particularly in the United States. We can roughly estimate the number of people who call themselves Muslim based upon the total population of a country, but to state precisely how many practitioners of Islam there are in any given country is not possible. Statistics about different religious groups provide us only with an estimate of those who claim to be adherents of different religions, and these statistics do not indicate the degree of religiosity and devotion to religious principles held by practitioners of any faith.

THE SECOND-LARGEST WORLD RELIGION

Nonetheless, it is not inaccurate to assert that approximately one out of every five persons alive is a Muslim. Islam claims at least 1.2 billion adherents, making it the second-largest world religion after Christianity. Muslims live in every corner of the world. Asia is home to more than 800 million Muslims, about 67 percent of the world Muslim population. There are large and concentrated populations of Muslims in Southeast, South, and Southwest Asia. Almost half of the world's Muslims live in the four countries of Indonesia, Pakistan, Bangladesh, and India. Muslims are the largest religious minority in Hindu-dominated India, where they account for more than 135 million people, or about 14 percent, of that country's population. There are significant populations of Muslim minorities living in China, the Philippines, and Thailand. Other large Muslim countries of Asia are Iran, Turkey, and Egypt, each of which contains more than 60 million Muslims. There are also significantly large populations of Muslims in the former Soviet central Asian countries of Kazakhstan, Uzbekistan, Turkmenistan, Tajikistan, and Kyrgyzstan.

There are more than 300 million Muslims living on the continent of Africa. Islam is the main religion of the North African countries of Egypt, Libya, Tunisia, Algeria, and Morocco. Muslims are also found in sub-Saharan African

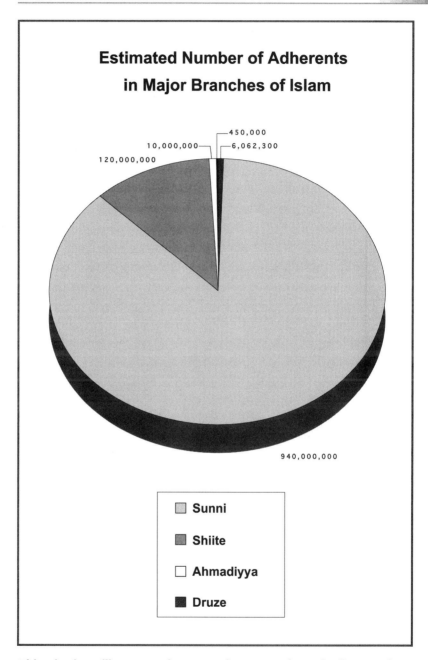

**Estimated Number of Adherents
in Major Branches of Islam**

450,000
10,000,000
6,062,300
120,000,000

940,000,000

- ☐ Sunni
- ☐ Shiite
- ☐ Ahmadiyya
- ☐ Druze

This pie chart illustrates the approximate number of adherents in each of the four major branches of Islam.

countries. The nation of Nigeria is home to more than 50 million Muslims.

In Europe, Islam is the second-largest religion after Christianity, with more than 20 million adherents. Countries such as Germany, France, Austria, and England contain large Muslim minorities. The only European countries with Muslim majorities are Albania and the nation of Bosnia and Herzegovina.

Muslims have lived in North America for several centuries, and today, there are about 6 million Muslims living in the United States. Mosques and minarets have become familiar cultural features in the landscapes of large American cities such as Los Angeles, New York, Houston, and Detroit, which are home to sizable Muslim populations.

BRANCHES OF ISLAM

Like Christianity, which divided into several branches after its inception, Islam also divided into two major branches, *Sunni* and *Shiite* Islam. Soon after the death of the prophet Muhammad in 632, Muslims fell into a disagreement about the legitimacy of his successors. Although a majority of Muslims accepted the decision of the powerful clan elders that Abu Bakr, the Prophet's close friend and father-in-law, would be his successor, another group of Muslims strongly believed that the succession should continue within the familial line of Muhammad. Because Muhammad did not leave a living son, this party chose 'Ali, Muhammad's cousin and son-in-law, as the legitimate successor to the Prophet to lead the Islamic community (*Ummah*). Their allegiance to Ali gave the members of this group the name *Shiite al-'Ali*, which means "partisans of Ali." Over time, the word *al-'Ali* was dropped from the name and the term used became simply *Shiite*.

Today, Shiites form approximately 15 percent of the total Muslim population of the world. They are scattered throughout the world. The two countries with Shiite majorities are Iran and Iraq. There are also a considerable number of Shiites living in Lebanon, Syria, Saudi Arabia, Kuwait, the United Arab Emirates, and Afghanistan. Iran is the largest Shiite country in the world—over 90 percent of the Iranian population belongs to the Shiite sect.

2

Muhammad

I have always held the religion of Muhammad in high estimation because of its wonderful vitality. It is the only religion, which appears to me to possess that assimilating capacity to the changing phase of existence, which can make itself appeal to every age. I have studied him—the wonderful man, and in my opinion far from being an anti-Christ, he must be called the Savior of Humanity.

—Sir George Bernard Shaw

MUHAMMAD, THE MESSENGER OF GOD

About 570 years after the birth of Jesus, in the city of Mecca (Makkah) on the Arabian Peninsula, a child was born who later became the last Prophet of the three major Abrahamic religions. The child was Muhammad and the religion that he revealed to the world was Islam. Today, more than 1,400 years after his birth, Muhammad remains the most respected religious, political, and historical figure for more than one billion Muslims throughout the world. He is known as the "perfect man," an ideal example of a father, husband, friend, judge, statesman, devout Muslim, and in general, a wise, kind, and generous human being.

Unlike many other prophets before him whose lives and works were wrapped in mystery, Muhammad's life is well documented. He is an authentic historical figure, and almost every event of his life was carefully recorded as he gradually developed from a sheep-herding orphan into a well-known messenger of God. For a better understanding of Muhammad and the impact of his message we need to look at the Arabian Peninsula as it was during the lifetime of Muhammad.

PRE-ISLAMIC ARABIA

Lying at the confluence of the three major continents of Asia, Africa, and Europe, the land of Arabia consists of vast deserts, some steppes, and oasis. A shortage of water has made a major portion of the peninsula uninhabitable. However, wherever water is available through surface or underground resources, life persists. For most of the peninsula's history, the inhabitants of Arabia have survived mainly through animal husbandry, small-scale agriculture, and some trade in major cities. The most livable parts of the peninsula have been the southern and western sections. In the south, Yemen, known as the Arabia Felix, was once the seat of the flourishing civilization of Sheba that is mentioned in the Bible.

The people of Arabia at the time of Muhammad practiced both settled and nomadic lifestyles. Although animal husbandry and agriculture were the primary sources of livelihood for many, trade was the occupation of the wealthy classes. The economically disenfranchised often resorted to raiding the many trade caravans, which made trade a dangerous business. Trade caravans traveled far beyond the Arabian Peninsula to distant lands, and carried merchandise to potential customers in places such as Syria, Egypt, Abyssinia (Ethiopia), Iraq, Iran, Sind (Pakistan), and Hind (India). The city of Mecca, where Muhammad was born, was the main trading center of Arabia.

Arabian society was tribal in nature. One's identity as well as one's protection came from his or her membership in an extended family. Several related families formed a clan, and a collection of related clans comprised a tribe. One's loyalty therefore was first to the extended family, second to the clan, and then finally, to the tribe.

The elders and leaders of powerful families and clans selected from among their members a man to become their tribal chief. The chief worked in close association with an advisory council (*majlis al-shura*) that consisted of a group of respected elderly tribal members. The main obligations of the chief and the advisory council were to preserve tribal solidarity, secure the tribe's financial and social well-being, and protect the honor of tribal members. Honor had to be defended at any cost. Codes of honor consisted of manliness as demonstrated in military skills and acts of bravery, nobility of character evidenced in expressions of hospitality and generosity, and family pride and genealogical superiority displayed through poetry, moral courage, and physical strength.

Kinship and tribal affiliations were indicators of unity and loyalty. There was no large-scale political unity. It was not unusual for different tribes to compete for power and control of the meager resources of Arabia; thus, intertribal warfare was common. The larger and more powerful tribes often raided the smaller ones and attempted to weaken and eventually reduce them to dependent client status. The most powerful tribe of Arabia at the time of Muhammad was the *Quraysh* tribe, which controlled the city of Mecca.

In terms of religion, most people of pre-Islamic Arabia were idol worshipers. They prayed to idols of their own invention and manufacture in various forms of gods and goddesses. These idols were often associated with sacred natural objects or places such as springs, wells, trees, and rock formations. Often these sanctuaries contained the graves of tribal ancestors and were carefully maintained and guarded by members of related tribes. The most important idols or deity-figures were kept in the *Kaaba*, a cube-shaped house or shrine in Mecca that, according to Muslim legends, was built by the prophet Abraham for the worship of God, the creator of the universe. By the time of Muhammad, the monotheism espoused by Abraham had been lost in Arabia and the shrine he established had become a sanctuary for more than 360 idols that were objects of worship and were considered the protectors of various tribes. The most important of these idols was the god *Hubel*, known as a war god. Hubel, along with *Al-Lat, Manat,* and *Uzza,* were the most-worshiped gods in Mecca. The relationship between these idols and the people of Arabia was based more upon fear than on love.

Due to the importance of the Kaaba, every year people from different parts of Arabia and neighboring lands made a pilgrimage to Mecca to circumambulate (walk around) the shrine. Based upon a "gentlemen's agreement" among the tribes of Arabia, no warfare was allowed during the months of pilgrimage. This allowed for peaceful periods that presented ideal opportunities for trade and commerce. Thus, the interrelationship between religion and commerce made Mecca the richest and most powerful city of Arabia.

The idols of the Kaaba were not only objects of worship but also valuable sources of income, especially for the powerful clans of the Quraysh tribe that controlled the city. Not all clans affiliated with the Quraysh tribe enjoyed the same levels of financial prosperity and political power. The leading clan at the time of Muhammad was the *Banu Umayyah* ("children of Umayyah"), which enjoyed considerable wealth and political power within the existing oligarchy. Muhammad belonged to the *Banu Hashim* ("children of Hashim"), a less powerful but nonetheless highly respected clan of the Quraysh tribe.

THE BIRTH OF MUHAMMAD

A few weeks before the birth of Muhammad, his father, Abdullah, died. Muhammad was very young, too, when he lost his mother, Aminah. Muhammad's grandfather sent him with a foster-mother to live among the desert Bedouins on the outskirts of Mecca.

As an orphan, Muhammad learned the skills required for traditional Arabian life, such as basic techniques of desert travel, survival, and self-defense. He also learned the pure Arabic language believed to be spoken and taught more properly by Bedouins than by city dwellers.

After a few years, Muhammad's grandfather died, and at the age of eight, Muhammad was given over to the care of his uncle Abu Talib. Because he was a poor child, Muhammad worked as a shepherd during his youth. Under the guardianship of his uncle, Muhammad started traveling with trade caravans, and soon learned essential trade skills.

By the time he was in his twenties, Muhammad had developed a reputation for integrity and honesty. He was well liked and respected by the people of Mecca, to the extent that many entrusted their valuable property to him for safekeeping. Due to his impeccable character, people referred to Muhammad as al-Amin ("the trustworthy") and al-Sadiq ("the truthful").

His reputation reached the ears of Khadijah, a wealthy merchant and a widow, who decided to hire him to be her business manager. Khadijah was delighted with the unusually large profit that he brought her after each caravan trip, and she was enchanted by his charm and personality as well. She proposed marriage to Muhammad. The twenty-five-year-old Muhammad was likewise attracted to Khadijah and accepted the proposal. According to legend, Khadijah was forty years old at the time of the marriage.

During their fifteen years of marriage, Muhammad and

Khadijah had a close and loving relationship. Khadijah was Muhammad's most significant supporter, especially during his early years of prophethood. They had several children together. The most famous of Muhammad's surviving children was Fatimah, who later married 'Ali, Muhammad's cousin. These two became among the most important personalities of early Islamic history.

PROPHETHOOD

Although idolatry was the prevailing religious belief in Mecca, there were a few people who had preserved the Abrahamic tradition of monotheism. These individuals were known as *hanifs* (or *hanafi*), meaning "rightly inclined." According to the Qur'an 3:67, "Neither was Abraham a Jew nor a Christian, but a hanif and a Muslim, and not an idolater."

Abraham, according to Muslims, had established the original ethical monotheism in Arabia, but gradually the monotheism of Abraham had been replaced by the polytheistic practices that prevailed in Mecca at the time of Muhammad. We have mentioned that Arabs of Arabia believed themselves to be descendants of Abraham's older son, Ishmael. Muhammad was considered the fortieth descendant of the house of Ishmael. Like his forefather Abraham, Muhammad was among the hanifs who were submissive to God.

Unhappy with the polytheistic and corrupt Meccan society, Muhammad often retreated to a cave in Mount Hira outside Mecca, where he meditated for many hours. In his pursuit of spirituality he pondered the prevailing cruelty, lustfulness, and materialism in society, brought about by ignorance. He was, in fact, in search of insight and the real meaning of life. In the lunar month of Ramadan of the year A.D. 610, during one of his regular meditations, Muhammad heard an angelic voice that commanded him to read. Muhammad, who had no formal education, replied that he could not read. The mighty voice, which Muhammad later identified as that of the archangel Gabriel, repeated, "Read in the name of your Lord Who created,

created man from an embryo. Read, for your Lord is most beneficent, Who taught by the pen, taught man what he did not know" (Q. 96:1–5).

According to Islamic tradition, on this night, known as "The Night of Power and Excellence," Muhammad, who was forty years old at the time, was chosen to become a messenger of God (Q. 97:1–5). This was the first of many revelations Muhammad received from God; he continued to experience revelations until his death in 632. Muhammad's compiled revelations are known as the *Qur'an*, a word that means "recitation." The reason for the name is that the texts were first revealed to Muhammad in recited form, and they were often recited by Muhammad and early Muslims. They continue to be recited by millions of Muslims throughout the world today.

Perplexed by his experience in the cave, Muhammad returned home to his wife, Khadijah, to tell her what had happened. Khadijah consoled him and asked for advice from her Christian cousin, Waraqah. After he heard about Muhammad's experience, Waraqah reassured Muhammad that he, like Moses and Jesus, had been called by the archangel Gabriel to become the new messenger of God.

Khadijah accepted Muhammad as a messenger of God and was the first convert to believe in God's revelations to Muhammad. Among Muhammad's other initial converts were the young 'Ali (his cousin), and Abu Bakr, who later became the first successor, or caliph, of Muhammad.

During the ensuing years, Muhammad found more followers. He preached submission to the one true God (Allah) and warned the people of Mecca against the practice of idolatry. Muhammad and his followers worshiped God at the Kaaba, which they considered the shrine of monotheism built by Abraham. They were, however, disturbed by the great number of idols kept there. As the first Muslims' message against idolatry and intention to remove the idols from the Kaaba became more aggressive, leaders of the Quraysh began to see Muhammad and his followers as a significant threat to the established economic,

AHADITH, OR SAYINGS OF THE PROPHET

The prophet Muhammad is a role model for devout Muslims. After the Qur'an, the Prophet's sayings are the most important source of moral guidance for the faithful. The following is a collection of sayings attributed to the Prophet:

"The first thing created by God was the intellect."

"The most excellent Jihad is that for the conquest of self."

"The ink of the scholar is more holy than the blood of the martyr."

"One learned man is harder on the devil then a thousand ignorant worshipers."

"Search for knowledge even if it takes you to China."

"Searching for knowledge is obligatory for every Muslim man and Muslim woman."

"Riches are not from an abundance of worldly goods, but from a contented mind."

"Reflect upon God's creation but not upon His nature or else you will perish."

"He who wishes to enter Paradise at the best door must please his mother and father."

"No man is a true believer unless he desires for his brother that which he desires for himself."

"Heaven lies at the feet of mother."

"The most perfect in faith amongst believers is he who is best in manner and kindest to his wife."

"Women are the twin-halves of men."

"The thing which is lawful, but disliked by God, is divorce."

"Actions will be judged according to intentions."

"Yield obedience to my successor, although he may be an Abyssinian [Ethiopian] slave."

"Assist any person oppressed, whether Muslim or non-Muslim."

"The creation is like God's family, the most beloved unto God is the person who does good to God's family."

"Modesty and chastity are parts of the Faith."

Source: These and other sayings of the prophet Muhammad are available online at "Sayings of the Prophet," *The Wisdom Fund*, http://www.twf.org/Sayings.html.

religious, and social order. When Muhammad and his followers announced their call to Islam publicly, they became subjects of persecution, torture, isolation, and boycotts by the leading Meccan oligarchy.

When the persecution of Muslims became overwhelming, Muhammad sent some of his disciples to the Christian kingdom of Ethiopia. The Ethiopian king, after allowing the Muslim refugees to explain their faith, decided the basic beliefs of Islam were similar to those of Christianity, and welcomed the Muslims as new immigrants. His refusal to hand over the early Muslim refugees to the Meccan leaders infuriated the Meccan oligarchy and resulted in the further persecution of Muslims in Mecca.

The worst years came when Muhammad lost his beloved wife, Khadijah, and his affectionate protector uncle Abu Talib. With the loss of these two loved ones and the increasing persecution he and his followers faced, Muhammad felt it necessary to find a more secure city. In his attempt to negotiate with the leaders of the nearby city of Ta'if (in present-day western Saudi Arabia), he was stoned and driven away by Ta'if residents.

In 622, when the situation looked hopeless for Muhammad and his disciples, a delegation from the city of Yathrib, located over two hundred miles north of Mecca, approached Muhammad and asked him to act as an arbiter and counselor between two warring tribes of their city. Muhammad understood the significance of such an opportunity and announced his agreement—only upon the conditions that his followers be permitted to immigrate to Yathrib and that the people of Yathrib accept Islam as their religion and Muhammad himself as the messenger of God. The delegation, aware of Muhammad's wisdom and skills in arbitration, accepted these conditions. Muhammad's followers began moving to Yathrib in small groups in order to avoid harassment by the Meccan leaders. Muhammad was the last to go to Yathrib. There, he received a warm reception from his followers who had been awaiting his arrival.

The year 622 in Islamic history became known as the year of *hijrah*, or "migration." It was in this year that the first true

Islamic community (*ummah*) was formed in Yathrib, and, due to the importance of this event, this year marks the beginning of the Islamic calendar. The name of *Yathrib* was later changed to *Medinat al-Nabi*, which means "the city of Prophet." Today, the city is known as Medina; it is the second most sacred city in Islam after Mecca.

Medina held the first *ummah*, or "Islamic community," a community that was religio-political in nature. Muhammad was the political as well as spiritual leader of this community. He was a messenger of God as well as a statesman. Religion and politics were intertwined from the very beginning of Islam, and Muhammad, and Medina exemplified this interconnection. Medina offered a union of church and state without significant distinctions between religious and secular domains. Muhammad implemented the rules of God based upon a combination of received revelations, his own wisdom, and Arabian traditions.

One of the most significant changes brought by Muhammad was to change the notion of community identity from kinship and tribal ties to common religious faith and commitment. He taught that human actions were not supposed to serve primarily one's self or tribal interests but to satisfy the will of God. Unlike pre-Islamic Arabia, in which familial nobility was a sign of prestige and superiority, in the new Islamic community it was the integrity and piety of a person that gave the individual significance. Tribal societies with their human-made laws were replaced by a religion-based society governed by divine law.

Although the new Muslim community flourished in Medina, Mecca was still alive in the hearts of the immigrants. New revelations in Medina increased the religious significance of Mecca by designating it as the new *qiblah* (direction of daily prayers) and place of *hajj* (pilgrimage) for Muslims. Before this, Muslims faced Jerusalem during their daily prayers.

The conflict between Muslims and the Meccan oligarchy soon led to several full-scale battles. In the first battle, although the Muslims of Yathrib were significantly outnumbered, they defeated the Meccan Army. This decisive victory against all odds energized the Muslim community and made the people believe God was on their side. They lost the second battle, however, and Muhammad himself suffered some wounds in the fight. The following battles were not decisive.

By the year 630, the Muslims put together a ten-thousand-man army and marched toward Mecca. By this time, many Meccan leaders had already joined Muhammad's community, and the existing military force in Mecca had neither the willingness nor the strength to resist Muhammad and his followers.

Many Meccans feared that the Muslims would be vengeful and unforgiving when they reached Mecca, but under the guidance of Muhammad, the conquest of Mecca was peaceful and no blood was shed. Meccans were offered amnesty and were invited to accept Islam as their religion and to submit to the will of God. After years of preaching against idolatry, Muhammad entered the Kaaba, the Abrahamic shrine to the one God, in victory, and then destroyed the idols with his own hands.

The people of Mecca gradually accepted Islam as their religion and joined the growing *ummah*. A Qur'anic verse mentions this mass conversion: "When the help of God and victory come, you will see people enter the religion of God in crowds, so glorify the Name of your Lord and beg His forgiveness. He, verily accepts repentance" (Q. 110:1–3).

The peaceful conquest of Mecca and the tolerance and generosity demonstrated by Muslims encouraged the other hostile tribes of Arabia to accept Islam as their faith and Muhammad as their prophet. Muhammad lived to see all of Arabia become a land of Islam.

In the spring of 632, Muhammad made his last pilgrimage to Mecca and gave a farewell sermon, which contains the fundamental concepts of Islam:

> O People, lend me an attentive ear, for I know not whether after this year I shall ever be amongst you again. Therefore listen to what I am saying very carefully and take these words to those who could not be present here today.

O People, just as you regard this month, this day, this city as Sacred, so regard the life and property of every Muslim as a sacred trust. Return the goods entrusted to you to their rightful owners. Hurt no one so that no one may hurt you. Remember that you will indeed meet your Lord, and that he will indeed reckon your deeds. Allah has forbidden you to take usury [interest], therefore all interest obligation shall henceforth be waived. . . .

Beware of Satan, for the safety of your religion. He has lost all hopes that he will be able to lead you astray in big things, so beware of following him in small things.

O People, it is true that you have certain rights with regard to your women, but they also have rights over you. If they abide by your right then to them belongs the right to be fed and clothed in mildness. Do treat your women well and be kind to them for they are your partners and committed helpers. And it is your right that they do not make friends with anyone of whom you do not approve, as well as never to be unchaste. O People, listen to me in earnest, worship Allah, say your five daily prayers, fast during the month of Ramadhan, and give your wealth in *Zakat* [almsgiving]. Perform *Hajj* [pilgrimage] if you can afford.

Learn that every Muslim is a brother to every Muslim and that the Muslims constitute one brotherhood. Remember one day you will meet Allah and answer your deeds. So beware: do not stray from the path of righteousness after I am gone.

O People, no prophet or apostle will come after me, and no new faith will be born. Reason well, therefore, O People, and understand my words, which I convey to you. I leave behind me two things: the Qur'an and my Sunnah [example] and if you follow these you will never go astray.

All those who listen to me shall pass on my words to others and those to others again; and may the last ones understand my words better than those who listen to me directly. Be my witness, O Allah, that I have conveyed Your message to Your people.[1]

A few months after his return from Mecca, in June 632, Muhammad died in Medina. Many of his followers did not believe that such a man could die, but Abu Bakr, Muhammad's close friend and father-in-law, appeared in public and declared, "For those who worshiped Muhammad, Muhammad was dead, but if they worship God, God lives forever." He then reminded them of the Qur'anic verse that states, "Muhammad is only a messenger; and many a messenger has gone before him. So if he dies or is killed will you recant? He that recants will do no harm to God, but God will reward the thankful" (Q. 3:144).

3

Qur'an

. . . indeed, it is a reminder,
So whoever will remembers it.
It is in honoured scrolls, Exalted, purified,
Written by the hands of scribes Honoured, pious.

—The Qur'an 80:11–16

A t the core of Islam stands the Qur'an, the holy book of Muslims. For Muslims, the Qur'an is the word of God revealed to the prophet Muhammad through the archangel Gabriel (*Jibril*). It is the eternal heavenly book authored by no one but God. Although it had been revealed to other prophets in the past, it was revealed for the last time to Muhammad in its original form, as a source of guidance for humankind. The Qur'an was revealed over a period of twenty-three years of Muhammad's life as a prophet. Some of the verses were revealed in his hometown of Mecca, and some were revealed in Medina, where he established the first Islamic community and built the first mosque.

Qur'an means "recital" or "reading" in Arabic. Arabic, the language of the Qur'an, belongs to the Semitic family of languages, and it is the only language of ancient scriptures that still functions as a thriving language spoken by millions of people throughout the world. Because God revealed his message to humankind in Arabic, it is considered the sacred language of Islam. The Qur'an has been instrumental in the preservation of the classical Arabic language for over 1,400 years. Throughout the history of the evolution of the Arabic language, the Qur'an has been preserved in its original form as revealed to the prophet Muhammad. Today, Arab Muslims are as familiar with the language of the Qur'an as were the early Muslims.

The language of the Qur'an is considered flawless. Due to its style and elegance, as well as its sacredness, the language of the Qur'an has had an enduring literary influence in addition to its religious impact. It has kept the Arabic language uniform so that Arabs from different parts of the Arab world who speak different dialects still consider the linguistic style of the Qur'an the ideal, and apply it to their writings. Today in the Arab world, the classic style of the Qur'an is studied as a masterpiece of immense literary value along with modern Arabic in major educational institutions. In fact, the modern Arabic language has remained very close to its classical ancestor. This is mainly attributed to the significance of the Qur'an's language as the eternal word of God, which needs to be preserved by generations of Muslims during different periods of Islamic history.

The language and style of the Qur'an provide its readers with an uplifting sense of fulfillment in this life and desire for a lasting peace in heaven. The Qur'an evokes profound emotions and thoughtfulness by constantly referring the reader to the living signs of nature as indications of divine force and gratitude. It also contains analogies, symbolism, and stories that articulately demonstrate the gentle values of virtuous life by providing examples from the lives of individuals whose actions and beliefs brought significant changes to their lives and the lives of their communities. The Qur'an provides believers with a sense of moral destiny and meaning of existence as exemplified by narrations of historical accounts of nations as well as of individuals.

Although the Arabian Peninsula had a long tradition of affection for prose and poetry of all types before Muhammad, the elegance and wisdom of the Qur'an made it an exceptional work of literature as well as of sacred scripture. The quality of the Qur'anic verses recorded by Muhammad left no doubt in the minds of his followers that they were divinely inspired, especially because they were conveyed by a man who was known to be illiterate. Muhammad's honest and trustworthy character also helped convince his followers of his truthfulness with regard to his communication with the divine. In this way, the Qur'an became known as the miracle of Islam and made a significant contribution in attracting spiritually minded people to the message of Islam.

Qur'an was revealed to Muhammad through *wahy*, or "revelation." *Wahy* in Arabic also means "inspiration." According to the Qur'an, God does not speak to any human except through wahy, from behind a veil, or through a messenger sent and authorized by him (Q. 42: 51–52). The Qur'an was brought down by a trusted spirit (Gabriel) to inspire the heart, mind, and memory of Muhammad, from where it was promulgated in human speech and propagated throughout the world (Q. 2: 97 and 26:192–193).

To the Muslim faithful, Qur'anic verses are not the words of Muhammad but the very words of God. Once a verse was revealed to Muhammad through the archangel Gabriel, he memorized the verse and recited it to his companions, who in turn recorded it in writing. The recorded writings then were recited back to Muhammad to ensure that they had been written correctly. During Muhammad's time, paper had not yet been introduced to Arabia, so the verses were written on palm-leaves, stones, clay tablets, or other available materials. Many early Muslims, both literate and illiterate, memorized verses of the Qur'an and recited them to each other and in their prayers. As the Qur'an was revealed to Muhammad part by part, it was written down and its passages collected and preserved. The organization and sequence of the current Qur'an is believed to be the same as that the prophet Muhammad used during prayers, especially during the holy month of Ramadan, when he recited the entire Qur'an and shared it with other worshipers.

A year after the death of the prophet Muhammad, his close companion Zaid ibn Thaabit, who was present during Muhammad's final and complete recitation of the Qur'an, was assigned to record the entire book, to preserve it for future Muslim generations. Zaid, a well-known scribe who was famous for having learned the entire Qur'an by heart, worked rigorously to collect the authentic recorded verses. The completed Qur'an as we know it today was then given to Abu Bakr, Muhammad's successor and the first caliph (head) of the Islamic community.

After the death of Abu Bakr, the original copy of the Qur'an was given to his successor 'Umar, who in turn left it to 'Uthman, the third caliph of Islam. By the time of 'Uthman's reign (644–656), the Islamic domain had expanded far beyond Arabia, and there was a great need for authentic copies of the Qur'an. 'Uthman had four copies made, which were then sent to the major centers of the Islamic world. These copies became the standard Qur'an. No other version or compilation was considered authoritative, and that still holds true. Unlike the Bible, which has been passed down in different versions, there is only one authentic version of the Qur'an written in Arabic. However, because the original Qur'an was written in a special script that did not include vowels or diacritical points, slight variations arose based upon the pronunciations of some of the words. As a result, there is more than one possible reading that may change the meaning of a sentence slightly; however, these differences in meaning are not significant enough to create problems, and these types of variant readings are recognized as authentic by Muslims.

The Qur'an contains 114 chapters (*suras*) of unequal lengths. Each surah contains a number of *ayat* (plural of *ayah*), or verses. There are more than six thousand verses in the Qur'an. Some suras, including the 103rd, 108th, and 110th, consist of only three verses. Others, like the second, are over two hundred verses long. Although the Qur'an was revealed over a twenty-three-year time span, its organization does not follow any chronological sequence. Apart from the beginning chapter, the Qur'an's chapters are arranged approximately according to their lengths, with the longest first and the shortest last. This order has made it difficult for non-Muslims to follow the theme of each chapter. With the exceptions of the short chapters, each of the Qur'an chapters follows no clear theme. The chapters frequently shift from one theme to another. This, in a way, forces the reader constantly to ponder the ideas communicated by each individual passage.

The Qur'an is about four-fifths the length of the Christian New Testament. It contains many stories from the Judeo-Christian biblical heritage, especially those about Moses. However, unlike the Book of Exodus, which offers a sustained narrative, the Qur'an does not offer such detailed stories. Instead, it contains rules and regulations regarding the moral and legal duties of Muslims. However, it has nothing in it comparable to the law code that is the centerpiece of the biblical Book of Deuteronomy. Many verses of the Qur'an sound like sermons, but unlike the voice of the preacher heard in the Gospels, which is supposed to be that of Jesus during his ministry on Earth, the Qur'an is phrased directly in the voice of God.

Although the sacredness of the Bible for Christians is usually due to its text and content alone, for Muslims, the physical books themselves are sacred as well, and they are treated as such. Muslims do not touch the book with dirty hands or impure intentions: "This is indeed the honorable Qur'an, in a book well-guarded, which none shall touch but those who are clean, a revelation from the Lord of the worlds" (Q. 56: 77–80). Observant Muslims complete the ritual of ablution (washing of the body), which is required prior to performing daily prayers, before handling the book. Also, the book is not treated like any other ordinary book when stored or shelved: It is considered disrespectful to place a copy of the Qur'an under other books, and if space is limited, it is preferable for the Qur'an to be placed on top of or above all other books. Usually, the Qur'an is stored in a clean and elevated place that is inaccessible to house pets. The book should not be stored or read in places such as bathrooms, which are considered impure by many Muslims.

The revelation of the Qur'an was not a new event, although it was, of course, new in Arabia. According to Islamic tradition, God had revealed his book in the past to other prophets, including Moses and Jesus. Here, one might ask why, if God had already revealed his scripture to earlier prophets, was it necessary to reveal it again to Muhammad? Muslims respond to this by saying that, although there were other revelations, they were not sustained in their pure form. There was an unfilled need for an original and unaltered revelation. Muslims believe that the scriptures of the Jewish community (the Torah) and of the Christians (the Gospel or the Evangel) had been partially corrupted by human interpolations and alterations. Jews, Muslims believe, corrupted the message of God when they separated themselves from the rest of humanity by propagating their doctrine of divine election by God as "the chosen people." Muslims also believe that Christians deviated from the true path of monotheism by turning Jesus, the messenger of God, into a god himself (Q. 5:20, 9:30–33). Out of mercy for humanity, God once again revealed the original heavenly tablet, in the form of the Qur'an, to Muhammad and the people of Arabia. This divine text has been preserved unaltered and in its pure form by Muslims for over 1,400 years, and it will continue to be a source of guidance for generations to come.

TEACHINGS OF THE QUR'AN

As its central theme, the Qur'an emphasizes two principles: monotheism (*tawhid*) and social justice. Without adherence to these two principles, the Qur'an asserts, individuals and societies will fail to fulfill their religious and moral obligations. A person who submits to God (in other words, a Muslim) should observe these two major obligations to the creator God by proper acts of worship (*ibadat*) and by just interactions with fellow human beings (*mu 'amilat*). A Muslim is also responsible for being compassionate toward other living creatures and caring for his or her natural surroundings. Throughout the Qur'an, Muslims are encouraged to ponder and become careful observers of their own behavior and occurrences around them. The Qur'an steadfastly admonishes the early generations of Muslims to reflect upon their traditional ways of conduct and to reevaluate their unjust customs and traditions. The Qur'an provides the faithful with a code of proper conduct, which, as we will see, later became the foundation of Islamic law, or *shari'ah*.

Many Muslims cannot properly understand the intended meanings of the Qur'anic verses without using accompanied interpretations. In fact, the text has been interpreted since the time of the prophet Muhammad. Today, the science of interpreting Qur'an is an important part of Islamic scholarship. Scholars who interpret the Qur'an must have a sound knowledge of the classical Arabic language, culture, and the early history of Islam.

Although Muslims believe that the Qur'an is the word of God and that Muhammad was only a conveyor of that word, one can still see connections between Muhammad's life events and the Qur'anic verses. The verses revealed to Muhammad in Mecca are different in content and tone from those revealed in Medina. As Muhammad became more settled in his role as the messenger of

God and leader of the Islamic community, the short, powerful, and warning revelations of Mecca gradually gave way to the longer, calmer, more community-oriented revelations of the Medinan period.

Due to the importance of the chronology of revelations in understanding the Qur'an, the order of suras as they were revealed and the place where each revelation was received (Mecca or Medina) are usually included in the heading of each chapter. During his twenty-three years as a prophet, Muhammad managed the Islamic community in a way that became a model for future leaders of Islamic communities. Because of his own pious manner of living, he came to be viewed as the paragon who could demonstrate the way life should be lived. His life and conduct were inspiration for compiling and codifying books of *ahadith* (plural of *hadith*), which were narrations of the *sunnah*, or life of Muhammad. The Qur'an advises the believer to seek God's and the prophet Muhammad's guidance by stating, "O you who believe, obey God and the Messenger and those charged with authority among you. If you differ in anything among yourselves, refer to God and his Messenger if you do believe in God and the Last Day. That is the best and most suitable for final determination" (Q. 4:59).

SUNNAH AND HADITH

As Islam continued to spread throughout the world, various Muslim rulers and jurists felt the necessity to develop an established set of laws by which they could rule according to Islamic principles. Although the Qur'an was the most important source of jurisprudence they could use, they also wanted to emulate the leadership of the prophet Muhammad, whom they considered the ideal ruler and administrator. There was a need for an authentic collection of Muhammad's deeds and sayings for the purposes of moral and judicial reference.

Hadith, an Arabic term meaning "narration," refers to any narration of events that occurred under the leadership of the prophet Muhammad. This includes his deeds, sayings, and things that were approved by him. Since God's revelations to humanity ended with the death of Muhammad in 632, knowledge of hadith became extremely useful in answering questions about moral, legal, and religious issues. During his lifetime, Muhammad was known for his conflict resolution skills. Solutions that he articulated under different circumstances needed to be collected so they could be utilized for future conflict resolutions. Hadith literature that accurately reported the Prophet's life, sayings, and deeds became considerably important. Because of the practical nature of hadith literature, in addition to uncovering the life of Muhammad, some scholars included the sayings and deeds of his companions and successors as well. Thus, the term *hadith* in its broader sense applies to narrations of lives, sayings, and the conduct of Muhammad and his early Muslim companions and successors.

Sunnah is an Arabic term that means "tradition" or "example." It denotes the way Muhammad lived his life. Although *sunnah* and *hadith* are very close in their definitions (many scholars, in fact, do not differentiate them), the terms are not really identical in meaning. A *hadith* is a narration about the life of the Prophet and what he approved, whereas the *sunnah* refers to his lifestyle or example. For faithful Muslims, knowing about the Prophet's lifestyle and knowing what he did, said, and approved are equally important. The Qur'an speaks of the prophet Muhammad as the ideal example to follow by stating, "You have indeed a fine model [of conduct] for anyone whose hope is in God and the Final Day and who engages much in the praise of God" (Q. 33:21). Books of ahadith that portray Muhammad and his life are, therefore, the second most important religious scriptures of Islam after the Qur'an.

While there is only one authentic version of the Qur'an, there are several collections of ahadith. About two centuries after the death of the Prophet, the collection of ahadith became a systematic science administrated by scholars who were often appointed by the courts of the caliphs. There were numerous stories about Muhammad and his companions' deeds and sayings, not all of which were necessarily authentic. To judge the authenticity of these narrations, a system was designed by which the factual ahadith were distinguished from the fabricated ones. By using certain criteria, ahadith were evaluated and their degree of authenticity graded as sound (*sahih*), acceptable (*hasan*), or weak (*daif*).

To do this, two methods were used. The first method was to study the authenticity of a hadith by examining the narrator's biography. A narrator's character, integrity, trustworthiness, reputation for piety, intelligence, and possible biases about the reported topic were carefully examined. Then, if the narrator had not heard the report from the original source (i.e., the Prophet), then the chronological continuity of involved narrators all the way back to the original source was considered. This was done in order to confirm that there was an unbroken chronological chain connecting all narrators to one another without any interruptions or discrepancies. For example, we might read that a narration came from A, who said that he heard it from B, who heard it from C, who was in the presence of Muhammad when the Prophet said or did the thing in question. Thus, the job of a researcher was first to examine the biographies and trustworthiness of the A, B, and C narrators, and then to establish a working chronological chain (*sanad*, plural *asnad*) among these narrators that would be deemed acceptable. For further example, if research showed that the transmitters B and C did not live at the same time or that they had never met during their lifetimes, then the chain that purportedly connected these people would be considered broken. The hadith would be declared unreliable and therefore unacceptable.

In the second method of verification, a hadith or narration about a particular event or incident in the life of the Prophet was compared with the content of the Qur'an and other likely narrations about the same event. If any discrepancies between the hadith and the Qur'an were found, due to the sacred nature of Qur'an, the hadith had to be rejected. If the hadith conformed with the Qur'an, then it was carefully compared and contrasted with other narrations about the same topic. The researchers looked for existing similarities and discrepancies. If the hadith fit in well with other narrations about the same event or topic, then the hadith would be considered reliable and, therefore, authentic.

One reason for this peculiar sensitivity about ahadith was that, by the ninth century, there were hundreds of thousands of narrations about Muhammad and his life, many of which were at odds with each other. These included a large body of false ahadith. Some of these were pious fabrications by those who thought of themselves as good Muslims and rationalized their made-up stories as being in conformity with Islam and therefore good for Muslims. Some Muslims, though, created spurious ahadith for various reasons that ranged from self-aggrandizement to achieving certain theological, judicial, or political objectives.

After years of hard work sifting through the large volume of attributed narrations, those determined to be authentic were compiled into books of ahadith. Six collections in all were accepted as authoritative and valid for use in official affairs such as judicial cases. These were the collections made by al-Bukhari (d. 870), Muslim (d. 875), Abu Dawud (d. 888), al-Tirmidhi (d. 892), Ibn Maja (d. 896), and al-Nisai (d. 915). The collections of al-Bukhari and Muslim are considered by many the most authentic of the six. The compilation of ahadith ended by the middle of the tenth century, and no other collection dated afterward has been deemed authentic.

4

Worldview

So commemorate the name of thy Lord,
and devote thyself to Him with complete devotion.
Lord of the East and of the West,
there is no other deity save Him. . . .

—The Qur'an 73:8–9

THE CENTRALITY OF THE
INTELLECT AND REASONING

The archangel Gabriel appeared to Adam and said, "O Adam, I have been instructed to have you choose among three things; select one and leave the other two." When Adam inquired about his choices, Gabriel said: "Intellect, modesty, and religion." After a brief contemplation, Adam replied: "I choose intellect." When he heard Adam's response, Gabriel instantly commanded "modesty" and "religion" to depart. Refusing to obey, the two stood next to "intellect" and remarked that they were under instructions to remain with "intellect" wherever it might be. "So be it," Gabriel agreed, as he ascended to the heavens.

This imagery is a metaphoric hadith narrated by 'Ali ibn Abu Talib, as he heard it from his cousin and father-in-law, the prophet Muhammad. Islam, as hinted in ahadith, does not recognize any separation between religion, morality, and intellect. Indeed, to accept religion without using the intellect is not encouraged. The Qur'an constantly invites humans to utilize their intellects as their guiding light in the search for God: "We shall show them our signs in all the regions of the earth and in their own souls, until they clearly see that this is the Truth. Does it not suffice that your Lord is the witness of all things?" (Q. 41:53)

Although the Qur'an is God's revelation through scripture, God also reveals himself to us through nature and history, but it takes an active intellect to discern those revelations. God's providential signs, as the Qur'an reveals, are everywhere in the natural world, in the seasonal round of planetary and animal life, in the regular courses of constellations, and in history. However, to decipher these signs, we need to open our hearts and minds and ponder about the order of our universe and reflect within our own inner spiritual reality (Q. 30:8). The prophet Muhammad made it clear that, by knowing one's self, one can arrive at knowledge of God. The Prophet advised us that we should seek knowledge throughout our lives, and that seeking will eventually lead us to the truth.

Nowhere in the Qur'an does God ask for people to blindly accept his message. On the contrary, the Qur'an clearly indicates that there is no compulsion in religion (Q. 2:256). Human beings, according to Islam, have been created and endowed with a sound nature (*fitrah*), which is a reflection of divine nature. Our fitrah is the essence of goodness and our internal guidance system; it functions as our personal conduit to God. If we use our intellect properly and reflect upon our fitrah, as God and his prophets directed, our "Inner Light" will guide us to our source and our creator, God. What disturbs our relationship with God is when we do not acknowledge our fitrah, ignore our intellect, and void our reason. The Qur'an refers to those who do not use their intellect as the worst of all beings: "The worst of beasts in the sight of God are the deaf and the dumb, those who do not understand" (Q. 8:22).

THE ANATOMY OF INTELLECT

In an article titled "Intellect and Reason in the Islamic World-view," Babak Ayazifar reminds us of a hadith that illustrates the noble station of the intellect and reason in Islamic cosmology and worldview.[2] In this fascinating metaphor, Muhammad speaks of a brilliant oratory between God and the intellect. It is reported that Muhammad said,

> Verily, Allah (God) created the intellect from a treasured light, a light concealed within His primordial knowledge—one that neither a commissioned prophet nor an angel of proximity [to the Divine Throne] was aware of. He then ascribed to the intellect knowledge as its essence, cognition as its soul, abstemiousness as its head, modesty as its eye, wisdom as its tongue, kindliness as its purpose, and mercy as its heart. Allah then bestowed upon, and strengthened, the intellect with ten qualities: certainty, faith, truthfulness, tranquility, sincerity, gentleness, benevolence, contentment, submission, and gratitude. Then Allah (Exalted and Majestic) said to it: "Retreat!" Thereupon the intellect retreated. Then Allah said to it:

"Come nigh!" Thereupon the intellect drew near. Then Allah said to it: "Speak!" Thereupon the intellect said: "Praise belongs to Allah, the one who has neither a foe nor a rival, neither a likeness nor an equal, neither a tantamount nor a similitude—the one before whose splendor every creature is submissive, humbled."

Then the Lord (Praised and Exalted) said: "By My grandeur and majesty, no creature have I originated more splendid than you, more obedient to Me than you, loftier in station than you, more eminent than you, or more exalted than you. It is through you that My oneness is acknowledged; it is through you that I am worshiped; it is through you that I am supplicated; it is through you that I am implored [by My yearning servant]; it is through you that I am desired; it is through you that I am feared; it is through you that My bondsman exercises reverent discretion toward Me; it is through you that I bestow reward; and it is through you that I apportion punishment."

Upon hearing this, the intellect sank to the ground prostrate, and remained in that state for a thousand years. Then Allah (Praised and Exalted) said: "Raise your head! And ask, so it shall be granted. Seek intercession, so it shall be accorded." Thereupon the intellect raised its head and said: "O my Lord, I beseech you to appoint me as an intercessor for whomsoever you have created me in." Then Allah (Majestic in His Might) said to His angels: "I summon you forth to bear witness that I have indeed appointed the intellect as an intercessor for whomsoever I have created it in."

This narration, as Ayazifar notes, exemplifies the high status of the intellect in the Islamic worldview. It is through intellect that one may reach the creator and it is intellect that acts as an intercessor between God and human beings. The appointment of the intellect as an intercessor is particularly significant, since Islam does not admit the possibility of intercession through any being other than God, save by God's leave. Even the prophets, according to Islamic literature, cannot intercede between God and humanity. Intellect, therefore, in the sight of God, occupies a position even higher than the positions enjoyed by prophets.

HUMANKIND AS GOD'S VICEGERENT

After the creation of the human from dust, God breathed his spirit into him and raised him above all other creatures (Q. 15:26–50). By breathing his spirit into the human, God provided him with God-like faculties and knowledge of creation that non-humans did not possess. If the human utilizes these faculties judiciously, then he can serve as God's vicegerent (administrative deputy) on Earth (Q. 2:30; 17:70). Of course, according to the Qur'an, God gave human beings a choice as to whether to accept the responsibility of becoming his caliph or vicegerent on Earth. When offered the challenge, the human accepted a task that all other created beings refused to take upon themselves: "We did indeed offer the Trust [of divine responsi-bilities] to the Heavens and the Earth and the Mountains, but they refrained from bearing the burden, and were afraid of it. But Man undertook it, he was indeed unjust and foolish" (Q. 33:72). Here we see that the Qur'an is ironic about the human's courage, free will, and amazing confidence to accept such a gigantic task by referring to him as a fool. To be God's true representative and vicegerent requires God-like qualities, and God is well aware of our shortcomings, especially when it comes to justice; therefore, he refers to the human as unjust.

The "Trust" was betrayed by a portion of the human race who became hypocrites and unbelievers and treated the earth and one another unjustly. There are frequent references in the Qur'an to nations that went astray and brought God's punishment upon them, contrasted with those who followed the path of God, remained faithful to their covenant, and received God's grace (Q. 30:2–10).

God gives human beings plenty of help in succeeding as his vicegerent by providing them with advice about managing the environment based upon moderation, balance, and preservation.

The Qur'an calls Muslims the Middle Path community, the path between extremes (Q. 2:143). Within the balance of creation, every being has inherent values as a spiritual and/or material resource. It is the human's duty as God's vicegerent to preserve this sense of balance by using the earth's resources sustainably

KINDNESS TO ANIMALS

As vicegerents of God, humans are responsible for the well-being of all creatures. Muslims have many traditional stories about kindness to animals, of which the following are a sampling:

- The prophet Muhammad said: A man walking along a path saw a dog with its tongue hanging out, trying to lick up mud to quench its thirst. He filled his shoe with water and gave the dog a drink. Because of this compassionate act, God forgave the man's sins. The Prophet was asked: ". . . Are we rewarded for kindness towards animals?" He said, "There is a reward for kindness to every living being."

- A cruel woman was not giving her cat food or water, and shut the cat out of the house. A neighbor who felt sorry for the cat took the cat and would not give it back to the cruel woman. They took their argument to the Prophet to be settled. After promising to look after the cat properly, the cruel woman was allowed to take back the cat. It soon became clear, however, that she had lied. Her cruelty toward the cat continued until one of Muhammad's companions cried, "What a terrible thing to do," and "What a very cruel and wicked woman!" Muhammad told his companions that "a great sin had been committed because one of Allah's creatures had been ill-treated; the woman who had treated her cat so cruelly will not be forgiven for her sins; she will be sent to Hell for her wrongdoing."

- Muhammad is quoted as saying, "He who takes pity on a sparrow and spares his life, God will be merciful to him on the day of judgment."

and avoiding greed, affluence, extravagance, and waste that will disturb the balance.

THE CONCEPT OF SATAN

Although humans are created initially by God in the best shape or stature, we can easily fall to the lowest depths if we allow temptations to undermine our *fitrah,* or divine nature (Q. 95:4–6). From the dawn of creation, human beings have faced an archenemy known as Satan, or *Iblis,* as he is called in the Qur'an. When God appointed human beings as his vicegerent and commanded the angels to prostrate themselves before them, all obeyed except for Lucifer (who became known as Satan). Satan failed to realize the human's God-given faculties, and saw only the lower nature of humans, seeing humans as potentially wicked and sinful, since they are made of humble clay. When asked by God why he refused to honor the human, Satan replied that he who was made of fire would not prostrate himself before a being that was made of clay. God was outraged by Satan's arrogance, jealousy, and disobedience, and expelled him from paradise and inflicted a curse upon him until the Day of Judgment. Disappointed about his fall from grace, Satan vowed that he would use all his abilities to tempt the weak among humans into disobeying God as long as the human lives on Earth. God intervened, saying that Satan could have authority only over those who would follow him. God was confident that his faithful servants with good judgment would not succumb to Satan's temptations (Q. 15:30–42). Satan's refusal to accept the human's higher status led to a constant challenge for humanity, a challenge of not allowing ourselves to be tempted by Satan and the forces of evil.

NO ORIGINAL SIN

Satan put his energy to work, and, as is demonstrated in another Qur'anic allegory, he tempted Adam and Eve to disobey God and to eat the fruit of a forbidden tree. When God expressed his disappointment about Adam and Eve's disobedience, they repented. God, "the Compassionate and the Most Merciful," accepted their repentance and guided them to the straight path (Q. 20:116–122). It is at this point in the story common to both Christian and Jewish traditions that we see that the Islamic explanation of humanity's fall from grace is different from that of the religions that preceded Islam. There is no original sin in Islam. Adam and Eve alone disobeyed God, and that act of disobedience was their own sin; therefore, they alone were responsible for their actions. God considered what they did a normal act of disobedience, and when he heard their sincere repentance, he forgave them. In sharp contrast, in the Judeo-Christian version of the events, the whole of humanity suffers for the sinful actions of Adam and Eve. All humans are born with Adam and Eve's sin—original sin—on their souls. In Islam, there is no concept of original sin. Muslims believe sin is not a state of being, and that humans have the free will to avoid sin by following the right path of religion. According to Islam, every child is born innocent and has no need to be saved or born again.

WOMEN ARE NOT AT FAULT

Another difference in the Qur'anic account of the creation is that Eve—and women in general—are not blamed for the fall. In the Qur'an, Adam and Eve are both blamed for their disobedience. Subsequent generations of women do not face shame, disgrace, and hardship because of Eve's temptations. The pains of childbearing and monthly menstruation are not women's punishment for the fall (as described in Genesis 3:16–18). They are simply facts of life, the condition of humanity.

In Islam, the greatest sins are refusal to submit to God and associating another being as a divine partner, which is known as *shirk*. It is arrogance and ingratitude that causes people to turn away from their creator and sustainer and to become *mushrik* (those who commit the sin of shirk). Shirk is a refusal to recognize one's higher spiritual being or *fitrah*, the guiding light toward ultimate truth. In the absence of a struggle to realize God as one and only and one's spiritual ultimate, a person becomes idolatrous (*mushrik*) by worshiping false icons such as power, fame, wealth, greed, and carnal pleasure—icons that degrade our natural desires. The Qur'an warns those who are succumbing to their lower, selfish desires: "You are obsessed by greed for more and more until you go down to your graves. Nay, in time you will come to understand when you behold hell-fire, and on that day you will most surely be called to account for seeking pleasure [in piling up things]" (Q. 102:1–8).

FOUNDATIONS OF ISLAM

"O you who believe! Believe in God and His Messenger and the Book which He has revealed to His Messenger and the Books which He has revealed before. Whoever denies God, His angels, His Books, His messengers and the Last Day has gone far, far astray" (Q. 4:136).

According to this Qur'anic verse, the core beliefs of Islam are believing in one God, in God's angels, in books of revelations, in the prophets, and in the Day of Judgment. These articles of Islamic faith are described briefly below.

Monotheism (*Tawhid*)

The centermost creed of Islam is *tawhid*, or the oneness and uniqueness of God. Tawhid is the first doctrine of Islam, and it is an indication of divine unity. According to this doctrine, there is no god but the one true God, a declaration of monotheism that is repeatedly recited during Muslims' daily prayers. The phrase *La ilaha illa'llah* ("There is no deity but God") forms the essence of Islam. In Arabic, *ilah* means any deity or god, whereas *Allah* (or *al-ilah*) refers to the "One and Only God." Although different Muslim nations may have their own terms for God (e.g., God is called *Khoda* in Persian), *Allah*, the Arabic term, is the most preferred name used by Muslims because in the Qur'an, God refers to himself as *Allah*.

Allah is the same God worshiped by Jews and Christians. He is the God of Adam, Noah, Abraham, Moses, Jesus, and Muhammad. He is also the one and only God and the eternal God. He did not beget another, nor was he begotten by another being, and nothing is equal to him. God has no partner or associates (Q. 4:48) and is not a Trinity (Q. 5:75–76). He is transcendent, omnipotent, omniscient, and has supreme authority over all that exists. He possesses limitless power and is the creator and controller of the universe. Eyes cannot see him but he can see all eyes, and he is aware of all secrets. Although humans cannot see him, God is nearer to them than they can possibly imagine: "We created man, and surely know what dark suggestions his soul makes to him, for We are nearer him than (his) jugular vein" (Q. 50:16).

According to the Qur'an, mercy and compassion are God's principal qualities. God is characterized this way frequently in the Qur'an, and, in fact, every chapter in the Qur'an except the ninth begins with the phrase "In the name of God, Most Compassionate, Most Merciful." This is a widely used phrase throughout the Islamic world, and many faithful Muslims begin their letters, articles, and public speeches with this phrase. By doing so, they remind themselves and their audiences that all things are in the hands of God and that it is his mercy and grace that allows them to do well in whatever they are pursuing. Many Muslims also recite the phrase when they start the activities of

THE STORY OF NOAH

Noah is an important prophet whose story appears in both the Qur'an and the Bible. Some time after creating humans, God became so dismayed at their corruption that he decided he had to destroy them. However, Noah was so righteous and devoted to God that God warned him of the coming disaster. He told him to build an ark to save his family and certain animals from the floods he would soon send to destroy every other living thing. Noah tried to warn the people to repent and return to God, but they called Noah a liar and ridiculed him while continuing to scorn God. As God promised, the floods came and Noah was safe while every thing else on Earth was swallowed by water. After the destruction was complete, the waters receded and the ark rested on a mountain. Noah lived and prospered for many more years in God's favor.

their daily routine, including eating, driving, and especially, activities that involve some degree of risk. They ask for God's compassion and mercy to finish the tasks they start.

While being forgiving and merciful, however, God does not forgive those who shirk or negate his existence and oneness unless they sincerely repent (Q. 4:48, 3:13). Nonetheless, even in these cases, God's mercy is limitless, as indicated by this humorous hadith: A man accused of denying God's existence was brought to the prophet Muhammad for trial. When the Prophet inquired about the case, he was told that the man, who had become despondent over a personal tragedy, was found in the desert throwing his spear into the sky while screaming that he wanted to kill God for unjustly inflicting a great tragedy upon him. After hearing the case, the Prophet stated, "Is it not enough that he acknowledged the existence of God by wanting to kill him?" The man was then set free.

Perhaps the most telling phrase Muslims use to indicate God's greatness and absolute power is *Allah-hu Akbar*, or "God is the Most Great." This phrase emphasizes the absolute power of God over all things. It is regularly used as a preface to daily calls to prayers. It was (and still is) shouted by Islamic soldiers during military exercises and combats. It is also used as a response to someone's expression of arrogance and egoism as well as a reaction to viewing an amazing phenomenon. In all cases, it is a reminder of God's complete power over all living beings.

Application of Tawhid to Everyday Life

A Muslim who submits to the will of Allah releases himself from all other obligations, except those that are conditioned to the terms of submission. His or her obligations are defined within the context of the faith and the things that will please (or at least not disappoint) God. He or she derives all his strength, energy, and inspiration from his or her willfully chosen master, God. By becoming devoted to only one benevolent master, the Muslim is liberated from all possible false masters. His or her aspirations and fears are directed toward pleasing God. The belief in a true master frees the Muslim from becoming a slave to others either out of fear or in the hope of gaining favor.

On the other hand, a person who does not submit to God often becomes a slave to false masters, or, as often happens in a spiritually challenged world, a slave to his or her own ego. When this happens, a person wrongfully strives for worldly pleasures such as power, fame, fortune, and desires of the flesh. A society full of people like this eventually turns chaotic and amoral.

The concept of tawhid also inculcates in the believer a realization of the unity of humankind. A believing Muslim rejects any notion of discrimination based upon racial and ethnic differences. All human beings, according to Islam, are children of God and they all stand equal in his sight, regardless of their ethnic background, gender, age, or color of skin (Q. 49:13). The unity of God also encompasses the unity of all of creation, the entire universe. There is absolute harmony in God's creation, and the perfect symmetry of nature and the complete order of planetary systems leave the believer with an impression that God has to be a mighty creator and governor (Q. 67:1–4). In the believer's mind, the concept of tawhid therefore comprises the unity of God, humankind, and the universe.

God, the universe, and humankind are all interrelated. Islam prescribes guidelines that regulate these intertwining relationships. A series of accepted codes of conduct decreed by Islamic law governs these relationships and establishes principles of justice and a basis for accountability to God. Islamic laws also formulate the framework for permissible economic, social, and political systems. As a law-oriented religion, Islam provides legal standards as well as spiritual incentives to guarantee fairness and justice for all involved in these relationships.

Angels

According to Islamic tradition, angels are imperceptible spiritual beings who are guided by God to administer to the universe and its intricate system of laws. Unlike humans, angels are free of sin because they lack the free will to be tempted by Satan. They are totally subject to the will of God and carry out his commands without the slightest deviation from their duties. Angels are created out of light but they are neither divine nor worthy of worship. In the hierarchy of the universe, the human was given a higher status than that of the angels when God commanded the angels to prostrate themselves before the human, prior to the divine appointment of the human as his vicegerent on Earth.

According to Islamic tradition, invisible angels surround and protect us. As our guardians, they are with us and attached to us, and they carefully observe our behavior (Q. 82:10–12). Angels are immortal and sexless, and they function as guardians, recorders of our deeds, and messengers from God to chosen individuals. According to tradition, each of us has two angels assigned to record our actions—good deeds and misdeeds (Q. 50:17). On the Day of Judgment, they will present these records when we go on trial before God. In the Qur'an, some angels, such as Jibril (Gabriel), Mikhail (Michael), Israfil, and Israel, are mentioned as archangels, each of whom governs a host of other angels. Jibril is the angel who revealed the Qur'an to the prophet Muhammad.

With God's will, angels can appear in the form of a human. According to a hadith, once, when the prophet Muhammad was sitting with his companions discussing religious issues, a fresh-looking stranger in immaculately clean clothing entered the mosque, gently approached the assembly, and started to ask thoughtful questions about the nature of Islam. When he finished his questions, he quietly departed. The companions of Muhammad were amazed by the sudden appearance and disappearance of a complete stranger who must have traveled a long distance to reach the mosque. When he noticed his companions' amazement, the Prophet informed them that the man was the archangel Gabriel, who had come to observe their session. Some of Muhammad's companions immediately ran after the stranger, but could find no trace of him. After an inquiry, it became clear that no one in the town had seen the person who had visited the mosque.

Jinns

In addition to humanity and angels, another being, known as a *jinn*, inhabits the Islamic universe. Jinns are intelligent, invisible spirits made of fire (Q. 55:15). Like humans, they enjoy free will, and therefore, they can be either good or bad. They have the capacity to take on human or animal forms and can help or hurt human beings as well as each other, depending on their whim. According to one Qur'anic passage, a group of jinns, after listening to a Qur'an recitation by the Prophet, converted to Islam (Q. 46:29–31). Like humans, jinns will be judged based on their sinful or righteous acts. Perhaps the image in Western culture or in English that would most closely describe a jinn is the genie portrayed in English translations of tales from the popular book *The Thousand and One Nights*.

Prophets, Messengers, and Scriptures

Belief in God's scriptures and messengers are the third and fourth articles of Islamic faith. After appointing humans as his vicegerent on Earth, God promised humanity that he would send guidance through prophets and messengers (Q. 2:38).

Prophets guide people to worship God and to live righteous lives. According to Islamic tradition, the first human, Adam, was the primordial father of humankind, and also the first prophet. Adam is also considered the first Muslim because he deliberately submitted to the will of God. All other prophets who came after Adam were also Muslim prophets, and they, too, submitted to the one and only God and obeyed his commands. The Islamic tradition states that 124,000 prophets were chosen by God to lead the Muslim community to salvation at various times between the lives of Adam and Muhammad. According to the Qur'an, "There is not a nation but that a Warner [someone who gives warnings; i.e., a prophet] was sent to it" (Q. 26:208).

According to Islamic primary sources, the Qur'an and the ahadith, God had revealed his message to other prophets before to Muhammad, and some of these prophets had their own books of revelations. Among the books of the prophets that the Qur'an mentions by name as sacred literature are the Books of Abraham, the Torah of Moses, the Zabur (Psalms) of David, and the Injil (Gospel) of Jesus Christ. Although there is no known trace of the Books of Abraham in extant world religious literature, the other books have survived in Judeo-Christian scripture. However, the Qur'an states that the content of these books was gradually changed since their first revelations. By the seventh century A.D., according to Muslims, there was a compelling need for an intact copy of God's original revelation, which was revealed to the prophet Muhammad in the form of the Qur'an.

In Islam, there is a distinction between a prophet and a messenger. A prophet (*nabi* in Arabic) is someone who conveys the message of God to the people, encourages them to do good deeds, and discourages them from misdeeds. The prophetic message does not contain a sacred universal law, and it is presented to a limited group of people during a particular time in history. Jonah, Elijah, and John the Baptist were examples of prophets. A messenger (*rasul* in Arabic), on the other hand, is a prophet whose message contains sacred universal laws that are collected in the form of a sacred scripture. Moses and Muhammad are two examples of messengers. Every messenger is also a prophet, but any given prophet is not necessarily a messenger.

The Qur'an mentions twenty-six prophets by name, twenty-three of whom are well-known biblical figures. Five prophets (Noah, Abraham, Moses, Jesus, and Muhammad) are considered the main prophets of Islam, and they are referred to as *ulu al-'azm*, or "the steadfast prophets of firm resolve" (Q. 46:35). Noah's tale in the Qur'an is very similar to the account found in the Old Testament of the Bible (Q. 11:25–49, 29:14). Abraham, as mentioned, is considered the forefather of Arabs, including Muhammad, the Prophet of Islam. He is also the first prophet who actively preached monotheism. The life and deeds of Moses were similar to Muhammad's in many ways. Moses is mentioned more than

two hundred times in the Qur'an, and his sacred scripture, the Torah, is comparable to the Qur'an (Q. 10:90, 79:15–25).

Jesus is another major prophet of Islam, and is considered a Muslim who submitted to the will of God. His birth to the Virgin Mary is fully described in chapter nineteen of the Qur'an, under the title of *Maryam*, or "Mary." His miracles of speaking in his cradle and healing the sick, his deep passion for helping the dispossessed, and his endeavor to feed the hungry makes Jesus a very amiable prophet in the Qur'an (Q. 3:45–47, 57:27, 61:14). The Qur'an speaks of Jesus as a messenger of God who invited his followers to worship God rather than worshiping him: "God is my Lord and your Lord, so worship him, therefore, this is the straight path" (Q. 3:51).

In Islam, any type of anthropomorphism (assigning human-like qualities to the nonhuman, such as God), including the Christian concept of the Trinity, in which God the father, Jesus the son, and the Holy Spirit are all aspects of the same god, is considered a deviation from the true path of monotheism. Jesus is considered neither divine nor a son of God by Muslims (Q. 5:116, 19:34–35, 5:17 and 72). According to the Qur'an, Jesus did not die on the cross, but was lifted up by God to heaven, and he will return to establish true justice on Earth (Q. 4:157–158, 43:61).

According to the following Qur'anic verse, Jesus heralded the coming of Muhammad (whose name literally means "The Praised One") to his followers: "And remember Jesus the son of Mary said 'O children of Israel, I am the messenger of God to you, sent to confirm the Torah that was before me, and I give you the good news of a messenger who will come after me whose name is Ahmad [the praised one]'" (Q. 61:6).

The Day of Judgment

The fifth article of Islamic faith is belief in the Day of Judgment. Like Christians, Muslims believe in life after death and the existence of heaven and hell. According to Islamic traditions, the life of this world and all that it contains will come to an end as a result of a cosmic cataclysmic event known as the Last Day (Q. 81:1–14). Only God knows when this day will come. All people and jinns who have lived on Earth since its inception will be restored to life to face their creator God and to answer for their deeds in this world. Those whose good deeds prevail will be rewarded and allowed to live happily forever in paradise (heaven), and those whose evil deeds prevail will be punished and subjected to live in hell, an abode of fire and torture.

This system of reward and punishment constantly reminds Muslims that life on Earth is transitory and always a preparation for the Day of Judgment. The ultimate responsibility and accountability of each person for his or her own actions is emphasized. On the Day of Judgment, each person's destination will be the outcome of his or her worldly actions. No redemption, atonement, or intercession through intermediaries will be accepted.

The Qur'an vividly describes the human's accountability on the Day of Judgment:

> Say it is God who gives you life and later causes you to die. It is He Who will gather you all on the Day of Resurrection. Of this there is no doubt, yet most men do not know it. It is God Who has sovereignty over the heavens and the earth. On the day when the Hour of Judgment strikes, those who have denied His revelations will assuredly lose all. You will see every nation on its knees. Every nation will be summoned to its Book, and a voice will say: "You will this day be rewarded for your deeds. This book of Ours speaks with truth against you. We have recorded all your actions" (Q. 45:26–29).

The Qur'anic description of the afterlife portrays a life characterized by spiritual as well as material rewards and punishments. Bodies resurrected to face judgment will clearly feel pleasures in heaven and pains in hell after they are consigned to their final destinations. The garden of paradise is described as a delightful place of perpetual peace and tranquillity with flowing streams, shaded trees, and exquisite gardens, a place where one can enjoy the company of his or her beloved ones (Q. 56:12–37). Hell, in contrast, is characterized as a torturous place of fierce blasts of fire, boiling water, and an everlasting canopy of black smoke (Q. 56:42–44).

5

Worship

O Allah! This House is Thy House,
and this Sanctuary is Thy Sanctuary,
and this Security is Thy Security,
and this slave is Thy slave.

—The Hajj Ritual Prayer

THE CONCEPT OF WORSHIP IN ISLAM

The term for "worship" in Arabic is *ibadah*. *Ibadah* is derived from the root *abd*, meaning "slave." According to Islam, God is the master and the human is the slave; *ibadah*, therefore, means "submission to the will of the master," who, in this case, is God. This is the same definition used for the term *Islam*, so we can conclude that worshiping God is the same as following the path of Islam.

For devout Muslims who submit themselves totally to the will of God, living on Earth is just a transitory stage. This life is a time for preparation for the Day of Judgment, to do what is necessary to pass God's judgment, after which we will enjoy eternal life in paradise.

God is constantly present in the minds and hearts of the faithful, and for them, worshiping and pleasing God are the main objectives of life. Worshiping God gives the lives of the faithful meaning. They consider this worldly life a testing stage, and they look forward to eternal life in which they can have lives of true peace and tranquillity. However, to reach that everlasting life, they have to work for it by worshiping God and following his commands as explained by *shari'ah*, or Islamic law. The faithful know they are responsible for all their actions, whether public or private, and they are well aware of the fact that God is omniscient.

WORSHIP IS LIVING A RIGHTEOUS LIFE

In Islam, worship is more than just the observance of certain rituals through prayer and participation in congregational events. Worship depends on how a person lives his or her life. Anytime a Muslim does something that pleases God, it is an act of worship. Worship is obedience to God. This obedience involves recognizing God's unity, and believing in angels, his prophets, the books of revelations, and the Last Day. It also entails a commitment to the Five Pillars of Islam—the five basic requirements for one to be considered a Muslim: the declaration of faith, daily prayers, almsgiving, fasting, and the pilgrimage to Mecca.

Belief alone is not enough to please God. Someone who truly submits to God needs to put his or her belief into practice by becoming a concerned member of his or her own community. A person's religious and social performances also need to be sincere, rather than mechanical. When Muhammad conveyed a revelation that commanded Muslims to turn in the direction of the shrine of the Kaaba in Mecca during daily prayers instead of toward Jerusalem, as the Muslims had been doing in the past, a group of Muslims took issue with the change. Another Qur'anic revelation then criticized the attitudes of those who performed the act of worship as a mere mechanical ritual:

> Righteousness does not consist in whether you face towards the East or the West. Righteousness lies in believing in God and the Last Day and the angels and in the scriptures and the prophets, and in disbursing your wealth out of love for God among your kin and the orphans and to travelers in need and to beggars, and in freeing slaves, attending to your prayers, and giving charity, and in keeping your promises, and in being steadfast in hardship and adversity and in times of peril. These are the ones who are true believers, and these are the ones who follow the straight path (Q. 2:177).

As the above verse indicates, in Islam, righteousness goes far beyond turning one's head toward Mecca or Jerusalem while praying. It is a person's compassion for the poor and steadfastness upon the straight path guided by the Qur'an and teachings of the Prophet that please God.

Since Islam is a way of life for believers, worship is living in accordance with God's will, in true submission to God. Every right act of a Muslim is considered an act of worship. For example, Muhammad stated that work may be considered a type of worship: "Whoever finds himself at nightfall tired of his work, God will forgive his sins." Muhammad also mentioned that seeking knowledge is one of the highest forms of worship: "Seeking knowledge for one hour is better than praying for seventy years." Simple daily activities, when they are done for the sake of

God rather than to please oneself, are acts of worship as well: "Receiving your friend with a smile is a type of charity, helping a person to load his animal is a charity, and putting some water in your neighbor's bucket is a charity." Even indulging in business activities and making money to feed one's family as far as it is done within the context of Islam is *ibadah*, or "worship."

The fulfillment of one's personal obligations, if done with God's satisfaction in mind, is an act of worship. According to Muhammad, the time that a man spends with his family is counted as an act of worship and he will be rewarded later for his kindness and attention toward his family. Even pleasurable activities, if done lawfully and with God in mind, are acts of worship. Muhammad's male companions were surprised to hear the Prophet say that having sexual intercourse with their wives was an act of worship. When he noticed their amazement, Muhammad continued by explaining that God wants believers to satisfy their desires; however, those desires have to be fulfilled within the framework of Islamic law.

The all-encompassing nature of Islam allows for a comprehensive definition of worship. Worship includes all constructive engagements by believers, so long as they are done for the sake of God. These activities may be either ritualistic, like prayers, or nonritualistic, like removing a harmful object from a public road.

RITUALISTIC WORSHIP

Emphasizing nonritualistic worship does not negate the importance of ritual worship in Islam. In Islam, as in other major religions, worship is conducted through a series of ritualistic acts performed at times individually and at other times communally. The most significant of these ritualistic acts of Islamic worship are the daily prayers, the fast of the month of Ramadan, and the pilgrimage to Mecca (*hajj*). These acts, in addition to the declaration of faith and almsgiving, form the Five Pillars of Islam, which will be discussed in the next chapter. Here we will discuss prayer as the most visible act of worship and the mosque as the primary place of ritualistic worship.

Prayers (*Salat*)

Among all rituals, daily prayers were the first to be instituted by the prophet Muhammad himself. Muhammad was known for saying that the one thing he cherished most in his life was the time he spent performing his prayers. Today, for true believers, prayer time is still a time of spiritual awakening and a moment to break away from everyday busy life to face God. It is a time for the rejuvenation of the soul, for reflection on one's life, and for remembrance of God as a beloved friend and guide. Adult Muslims are required to pray five times: at dawn, noon, mid-afternoon, sunset, and in the evening after dark.

Salat (prayer) is a highly formulized ritual and a very devotional act. It consists of a series of prescribed bodily postures that include standing, bowing (*ruku'*), kneeling, prostration (*sujud*), and sitting. Throughout the prayer ritual, the faithful must face *qiblah*, the direction of the *Kaaba* or the holy house of God in Mecca, the birthplace of Islam on the Arabian Peninsula. Each prayer contains cycles or units known as *ra'kats*. All daily prayers combined include seventeen ra'kats—dawn prayers have two ra'kats, noon and afternoon have four each, after sunset three, and the evening prayers four. Shiite Muslims combine the two noon and afternoon prayer rituals into one session and the two sunset and evening prayers into another session; thus, they pray three times daily instead of five times. Even so, they still perform seventeen ra'kats, just as Sunnis do.

Salat must always be preceded by a ritual of purification through washing, known as *wudu* ("making pure or radiant"). Wudu, or the ritual of ablution, involves washing one's hands and forearms to the elbows, washing the face, ears, mouth, and nostrils, and passing wet hands over the head and feet, or washing both feet to the heels. While performing the ritual of washing, one utters certain invocations for assertion of right intentions, purity, and guidance. In the absence of water, sun-cleaned sand may be used. The use of sand is allowed only when water is not available, and the ritual of using sand is known as *tayammum*.

If an individual has experienced severe impurities, such as sexual intercourse, menstruation, or direct contact with blood, dead bodies, or foul substances such as dog or pig saliva, then he or she must perform the ritual of *ghusl*, a complete ablution involving a ritualized washing of the entire body. Acts of ablution are very important aspects of worship in Islam. The Qur'an and sayings of the Prophet associate cleanliness with godliness.

Prayers contain fixed verses from the Qur'an as well as optional prayers. The heart and soul of the daily ritual prayers, however, is the opening chapter of the Qur'an, which is recited during all five required sessions. The sura (chapter) titled *al-Fatihah*, or "the Opening," contains the essence of Islam and clearly defines the relationship between humankind and God, and God and his creation:

> In the Name of God, the Most Gracious, the Most Merciful.
> Praise be to God, the Lord of the Worlds,
> The Most Gracious, the Most Merciful
> Master of the Day of Judgment.
> You alone we worship, and to You alone we turn for help
> Guide us toward the straight path
> The path of those whom You favored
> Not of those who have incurred Your wrath
> Nor of those who have gone astray (Q. 1:1–7).

Salat is both an individual and a communal act of ritual. It can be performed anywhere, but it is recommended to be performed in the mosque, especially at Friday noon. While in a mosque, believers line up behind the *imam* (prayer leader) and perform a communal prayer. Perhaps during the history of Islam nothing has bound Muslims together as effectively as the ritual of communal prayer. It is a soulful expression of unity by numerous believers who gather together, assemble in organized lines, follow a single imam, and recite the same Qur'anic verses while bowing and prostrating harmoniously.

Friday is the time for communal prayers. On this day, Muslims gather in mosques to perform congregational prayers. The

Qur'an emphasizes the importance of Friday congregations: "Believers, when you are summoned to Friday prayers hasten to the remembrance of God and cease your trading. That would be best for you, if you but knew it. Then when the prayers are ended, disperse and go your ways in quest of God's bounty. Remember God always, so that you may prosper" (Q. 62:9–10). Friday noon communal prayers are usually accompanied by formal sermons that deal with religious, moral, and political issues.

In addition to the required prayers, some very pious Muslims perform voluntary prayers. The very devout wake up hours before sunrise and, in the quiet of the night, offer prayers to their creator. These prayers are known as *nawafil*. Those who follow a spiritual path (*tariqah*) in addition to required prayers perform their own private prayers (*dhikr*), both in private and in communal forms.

The Mosque (*Masjid*)

The word *mosque* is a distorted version of the Arabic word *masjid*, which means "place of prostration." Mosques are houses of worship in Islam, and they symbolically represent the divine presence on Earth. Unlike Western cathedrals, whose architecture generally emphasizes verticality, mosques are usually built horizontally in a way that hugs the earth rather than ascends toward the sky. With the exception of a few features such as minarets, mosques usually are not very tall buildings. The architecture of Islamic mosques, however, is not uniform throughout the Muslim world, and designs are to a great extent influenced by the artistic taste of particular Muslims from various cultural regions as well as the availability of desired building materials.

As the main place of communal worship and prayer, the mosque is the religious symbol of any Muslim city. During the first few centuries of Islam's existence, a settlement without a major mosque was not considered a true city.

Mosques are usually located where they are accessible to city dwellers. The main community mosque is called the Friday mosque, or the congregational mosque. It is normally a relatively large building, often at the center of the city, and situated either along the city's main thoroughfare or very close to it. It is called the Friday mosque (*Masjid al-Jum'ah*) because the most important weekly community prayer is performed there on Friday at noon. It is also called congregational mosque (*Masjid al-Jame'*) because it is the main gathering place for believers. In traditional Muslim cities, before the advent of skyscrapers, the Friday mosque was the tallest structure in town and was easily visible— especially its tall minarets—from different parts of the city. Friday mosques today are usually within easy walking distance of where the majority of the population resides, and particularly is close to the shopkeepers in the bazaar.

Ideally, the mosque is the center of the city's spiritual life and blends well into the physical texture of the city. Unlike cathedrals that stand tall and separate from surrounding buildings, mosques are continuations of the crowded structures of the town and are often so contiguous with neighboring buildings that one cannot walk completely around the mosque. With the exception of especially distinct features, such as portal domes and minarets, mosques easily merge into their surroundings.

In some countries, such as Iran, the Friday mosque is often one of the main structures of the bazaar complex and, in many cases, is actually the focus of the bazaar, the center of large crowds and bustling activity. It is conveniently located at the center of the bazaar complex, where the majority of shopkeepers as well as their customers have easy access to it. Since Islam requires adult Muslims to pray five times daily, the shopkeepers and visitors need a mosque nearby at which to perform their prayers. Believers prefer to pray in a mosque because, according to a prophetic saying, prayers said in a mosque are twenty-five times more effective than those said elsewhere. Also, certain economic activities are deliberately carried on near the mosque to fulfill the needs of the house of worship's religious rituals and educational programs. Often, shops selling goods such as sandals, rosaries, perfume, candles, books, papers, and pencils are found near the mosque.[3]

In addition to its role as a place of worship, a mosque serves as a complex institution for educational, social, and political affairs. Mosques have also traditionally been favorite lodging places for poor travelers. Mosques are places where religious teachers meet with their students. Usually between prayer times, religious teachers give lessons either in sanctuaries or in the courtyard (if the weather permits). Religious teachers are also available to the common people of the community who come for spiritual counsel. Some religious teachers reside in mosques and teach the Qur'an and basic reading and writing to children who cannot afford regular schooling. Mosques usually have their own libraries, which, in many cases, include secular as well as religious collections. Formal religious education, however, is provided in institutions known as *madrasahs* (religious schools). Madrasahs are usually attached to great mosques or located very close to them, sometimes within the bazaar complex.

Mosques are also places where social and political occasions happen. From the early history of Islam, religion and politics have gone hand in hand, and mosques have functioned as places where people received news about events such as the distribution of government-subsidized goods, recruitment of soldiers for wars, taxation, leadership changes, and demonstrations.

A good example of mosques serving as political institutions can be found in Iran. The gathering of huge crowds at large mosques in Iran provides the potential for mass demonstrations, especially after emotional speeches by popular religious leaders during Shiite holy days, and makes the mosques a major factor in the unification of people who demand political changes. The role played by mosques in the 1979 revolution, which resulted in the fall of the monarchy and the establishment of the present Islamic Republic of Iran, is testament to the power of these institutions.

Great mosques have been constructed by royal families of different dynasties who ruled over various parts of the

Muslim world throughout history. The great mosques of Egypt, Turkey, Iran, and India are good examples of these royal buildings.

Today, some governments in Muslim countries, especially in the Middle East, are creating mosques with breathtaking architectural beauty. The building of mosques is also a sign of social prestige and an indication of the material wealth and

THE ISLAMIC CENTER OF GREATER TOLEDO

The first Muslim immigrants to Toledo, Ohio, came at the turn of the twentieth century from Syria and Lebanon. In the 1930s, a few of these early families established the Syrian American Muslim Society. It was not until 1954, though, that Toledo's first Islamic Center was built on East Bancroft Street, near downtown, to fulfill the needs of the Muslim community.

Over time, as many more Muslims came to the Greater Toledo area in the late 1960s and early 1970s, the Bancroft Street Center could no longer meet the religious and social needs of its members. After much deliberation and soul searching, it was decided to build a bigger, better facility.

In 1978, forty-eight acres of land were purchased in Perrysburg Township. The center's foundation was laid in October 1980, though actual construction did not begin until September 1982. The present center in Perrysburg was in planning for over a decade. Its classic Islamic architecture was the first of its kind in North America. The building officially opened on October 22, 1983. Two wings were added in 1991 to accommodate increased enrollment in the weekend school and to expand the social hall facility.

The present center is the culmination of the dreams and aspirations of the handful of Muslims who first migrated to this part of the United States some seventy-five years ago, and the many others who followed in their footsteps. Today, more than twenty nationalities are repre- sented in the center. In addition to fulfilling the religious and cultural needs of its members, the center provides an important bridge of understanding between its members and the community at large. As a result, the scope and purpose of the Islamic Center goes well beyond the typical objectives of a religious organization.

Source: Islamic Center of Greater Toledo, available online at *http://www.icgt.org/*.

religious piety of their builders. Small mosques, however, are constructed by average people, using money collected from a particular neighborhood, guild, or private donors. There is a hadith that states, "For him who builds a mosque, God will build a house in Paradise." This is a powerful encouragement for the building of new mosques.

Many mosques are built in residential areas. Political and community leaders, by building mosques, display their degree of religiosity. Neighborhood mosques are located at the center of each residential district, often along the bazaar route and next to a few other public structures. People of the neighborhood usually meet at the local mosque on a regular basis, and after performing the scheduled worship rituals, they may discuss problems related to their area, such as security, water, garbage disposal, loitering youth. Social and family affairs, including marriages, divorces, mourning, and celebrations are also discussed at local mosque gatherings.

Architecture of a Typical Mosque

The early mosques of Arabia at the time of the Prophet were plain-looking structures. As Islam spread throughout the world, though, mosques became more sophisticated in design. Today, there are mosques all over the world with various architectures and designs. Whatever the design of the mosque, however, there are certain features that are usually shared. Some of these features—such as minarets (towers) and domes— are visible from outside, while some are internal features, like the *mihrab* (prayer niche facing Mecca) and the *minbar* (raised pulpit seat).

Domes and minarets have become the symbols of the Islamic cultural landscape. The high dome-shaped structure of mosques with their numerous illuminated apertures is representative of the sky shining at night. In a way, mosques are supposed to be miniature representations of the universe, with a round blue sky embracing the earth.

Minarets are now regular features of mosque architecture,

although they were not part of the earliest mosques. As Islam spread into Syria, Muslims may have borrowed the idea of a tower from the Byzantine churches there. Minarets (the word means "light-giving") have several functions, including increasing visibility to make it easier to locate a mosque. They are also used for calling believers to prayers. In earlier times, before loudspeakers were invented, the *muezzin* (*muadhdhin*) ("crier") stood in the room at the top of the minaret and recited the *azzan* (*adhan*) to call people to prayers.

Every mosque has to provide a clear indication of the *qiblah*—the direction toward the Kaaba, the holy house of God in Mecca. The architectural feature in a mosque that points toward the qiblah is the *mihrab*; it is usually a niche in the wall. Here, the imam faces the qiblah wall while the members of congregation line up behind him in an organized fashion. Because it represents the direction of the Kaaba, the house of God, the mihrab is considered the holiest feature of the mosque. A mihrab is usually made out of masonry with pillars at the sides, and is often highly decorated. In many mosques, like those in Iranian cities, an elaborately decorated roof area made up of geometric shapes usually stands above the qiblah wall. The mihrab is also a later addition (from the ninth century) to the mosque, and was perhaps borrowed from Christian churches or Zoroastrian temples.

Minbars are pulpits usually located next to the mihrab. Those who give sermons or other speakers during Muslim services use them. The minbar of the prophet Muhammad had no more than two steps and a seat. Later on, the number of steps was increased to six, the number minbars have today. Alongside the minbar and mihrab in a modern mosque, one can see copies of the Qur'an and other books of prayers. Inside Shiite mosques are pieces of clay stamps (*muhr*) made from the soil of sacred places (such as Mecca); the faithful place their foreheads against these during prostration.

The floor of a mosque is usually covered with carpets. Due to strict Islamic opposition to idolatry, any representation of human or animal life is forbidden inside the mosque. As a result, geometric and flowery designs and especially calligraphy have been employed to decorate the walls and other parts of the mosque. Walls of traditional mosques are usually decorated with verses from the Qur'an or sayings of the prophet Muhammad written in exquisite calligraphy.

Administration of Mosques

Traditionally, mosques in Islamic countries have been financed by revenue received from endowments (*waqf*). Endowments are often agricultural lands, which are administered by the donor or the donor's family. For the large mosques, there has often been more than one endowment. Sometimes, in the absence of a donor, a judge or a representative of a judge oversees the financial affairs of a mosque. The imam may also sometimes serve as an administrator.

Rules of the Mosque

Before entering a mosque, a visitor should remove his or her shoes and leave them in designated shoe racks. In smaller neighborhood mosques that have no shoe racks, people leave their shoes by the entrance door. Also prior to entering the mosque, one needs to perform the ritual of ablution (cleansing), or *wudu*. Traditionally, there are pools with fountains in the courtyard of the mosque or a building attached to it to facilitate the ablution process. In modern mosques, one often finds hot and cold water faucets, along with stacks of towels.

Once inside the mosque, one should speak softly without disturbing the people who are praying. Performing two *ra'kats* of prayers upon entering is recommended. For Friday prayers with high participation, it is recommended that visitors wear nice clothing and perfume.

Women may come to the mosque, but they sit apart from the men. Often there are separate rooms that segregate men and women. If there is only one room available, women are supposed to sit behind the men in the room during prayers.

The reason for segregation is to avoid distraction. That is, it is believed that a woman worshiper can better concentrate on her prayers when she is not worried about attracting attention, for example, because the hem of her skirt may rise as she kneels.

6

Growing up Muslim

*The Messenger of Allaah
(peace and blessings of Allaah be upon him)
said: "Fear Allaah and be fair to your children."*
—Saheeh al-Bukhari

For a believer, Islam is more than a religion, it is a way of life. Islam is not confined simply to doctrines concerned with the sacred but recommends specific individual and societal acts, such as almsgiving, fasting, and pilgrimage, that bind a community together. Islam provides criteria for human interactions as well as interactions with God and natural surroundings. For a devout Muslim, therefore, Islam can be regarded as a religion of orthopraxy, meaning that Muslims act in specified matters in ways defined by religion. This is not to be confused with orthodoxy, that is, conformation to intricate doctrines set forth in texts formulated by scholars.

From childhood onward, Islamic values are instilled in the mind and heart of a believer, so he or she can have a sound grasp of good and bad within the Islamic context. A Muslim's religious training falls into two categories: acts of worship (*ibadat*) and human interrelations (*mu'amalat*), or transactions. While attending to prayers is an act of worship or ibadat, helping the poor and being honest in one's business affairs fall in the category of mu'amalat. Worshiping God without being concerned about the well-being of fellow humans is not enough to achieve salvation, as indicated in the verse: "Have you thought of him who denies the Last Judgment? It is he who turns away the orphan and has no urge to feed the poor. Woe to those who pray but are heedless in their prayer, and who make a show of piety yet refuse small kindnesses" (Q. 107:1–7).

EVERYDAY CULTURAL CEREMONIES
Birth Celebrations

Babies are considered gifts from God, and so their birthdays are a time for rejoicing and celebration. One of the first things Muslims do after a child is born is to recite the *shihadah* ("There is no deity but God, Muhammad is the Messenger of God") and some Qur'anic verses directly into the child's ears. Usually, a religiously respected person who is known for his or her piety performs this ritual.

Next, a proper name must be chosen for the baby. If the

parents are devout Muslims, the names chosen normally have some Islamic significance. For example, a child might be named after one of the prophets mentioned in the Qur'an or members of Muhammad's family and associates. In some countries, parents wait until the seventh day after the child's birth to announce the name. On the seventh day, family and friends gather in the home of the new baby's parents, where the name is formally proclaimed. Announcement of the name is usually followed by a feast, and later, by singing and rejoicing. Usually, the parents make charitable donations to the poor as a way of thanking God for the birth of the new child.

The Marriage Contract (*Aqd Nikah*)

According to the prophet Muhammad, "when a servant of God marries he fulfills half of his religious duty, to fulfill the other half he has to follow the path of Islam." Because of its obvious importance in a Muslim's life, a wedding is seen as a blessed act, and Islam wants young people to find their mate and marry as soon as they can afford to support a family and enjoy mutual love, harmony, and respect. Married Muslims are encouraged to have children and raise them as observant Muslims.

In Islam, marriage is viewed as a civil contract—not a religious rite. A wedding ceremony requires the consent of both parties and the presence of two adult witnesses in order for the marriage to be official. Since there is no priesthood in Islam, the wedding may be conducted by anyone who knows enough about Islamic law in regard to marriage. Usually, however, the presence of a religious teacher or preacher is desirable.

The man and woman being married verbally exchange the necessary vows indicating their commitment to one another and their total satisfaction with the terms of the marriage in the presence of their witnesses. It is customary (and religiously required) that the man provide his new wife with a marriage gift (such as money or the deed to a piece of property). This gift, known as *mehr*, becomes the property of the wife, and she may use it as she pleases. Of course, in happy marriages, the gift is used for the well-being of the entire family. After these required steps, the couple then signs the marriage contract and they are officially considered husband and wife.

This process outlines the minimum requirements based on Islamic law. However, for those who can afford it, a wedding is a lavish ceremony at which many friends and relatives are present when the couple exchanges vows. If the couple's families are strict about the gender segregation rules of Islam, then there will

WHAT IS *HIJAB* (VEILING)?

Faithful Muslim women are often seen in public wearing *hijab* in the form of a headscarf or a loose-fitting garment that covers their body's curves. Hijab is also called *burqah* or *chador*. The main reason for this veiling is modesty, as indicated in the Qur'an:

> Say to the believing men that they should lower their gaze and guard their modesty; that will make for greater purity for them; and God is well acquainted with all that they do. And say to the believing women that they should lower their gaze and guard their modesty; and that they should not display their beauty and ornaments except what must ordinarily appear thereof; that they should draw their veils over their bosoms and not display their beauty except to their husbands . . . (Q. 24:30–31).

Proponents of hijab argue that the veiling protects women from the gaze of men and prevents them from being treated as sex objects. Instead of focusing on their physical beauty, men search instead for their intellect and inner qualities.

There is no clear instruction about hijab in the Qur'an; however, there is a verse that some opponents of hijab argue is meant to be applied only to the wives of the Prophet, and not to all Muslims: "O Prophet, tell your wives and daughters and the believing women to draw their outer garments around them (when they go out or are among men). That is better in order that they may be known (to be Muslims) and not annoyed . . ." (Q. 33:59). Many modern Muslims believe that hijab should be the choice of women themselves, not something imposed on them by law as is done in Iran and Saudi Arabia.

be separate ceremonies for men and women. In fact, governments like those in Iran and Saudi Arabia impose gender segregation in all public ceremony halls. This has caused protest from members of the population who are not as observant of religious rules and prefer to have mixed ceremonies in which both male and female family and friends may participate.

Death Rituals

For faithful Muslims, death is not the end of existence; it is the continuation of the journey that will take them to meet their creator God. According to Islam, all human beings belong to God and to him they shall return. Muslims believe they will rejoin their loved ones in paradise if they follow the right religious path.

Since death is not seen as a finality, there is no need to remain in the state of grief for a long time after losing a loved one. Usually, family and friends gather in the home of the deceased or close relatives, where they express their sorrow and give consolation and comfort to the deceased's immediate family members. They recite verses from the Qur'an and pray for the soul of the deceased. Tea, coffee, and some sweets, such as dates, are often served.

The body of the deceased has to be washed carefully, wrapped in a white sheet of cloth, and carried to a mosque or other burial place for funeral prayers. A congregation made up of close relatives, led by a pious individual, conducts a short funeral service, and then the body is buried. The body is placed in the grave so that the deceased faces the qiblah, the direction of the holy house of God in Mecca.

LEARNING RELIGIOUS RESPONSIBILITIES

For a Muslim, moral conduct is a religious duty. When Muhammad was asked to define the faith, he replied, "Faith is a tree with over seventy branches, the highest of which is believing in the oneness of God, and the lowest of which is a simple act of removing a harmful object from the road." Removing a harmful object from the road is an act of *ihsan*, or a virtuous act (an act of doing good). Muhammad defined *ihsan* as "worshiping God as if you see Him, because even if you do not see him, He surely sees you." God is observant of all our deeds and aware of our intentions. Doing ihsan, therefore, pleases God and is considered the highest form of devotion to God.

Five Pillars of Islam

When Muhammad was asked to define the concept of surrendering to God (Islam), he responded by saying that surrender is:

1. To testify that there is no god but God and that Muhammad is the messenger of God (*shahadah*);

2. To perform the prayers (*salat*);

3. To give alms (*zakat*);

4. To fast during the month of Ramadan (*saum*); and

5. To make the pilgrimage to the holy house of God in Mecca (*hajj*).

Throughout the history of Islam, the five religious requirements prescribed by God through the prophet Muhammad have been known as the Five Pillars of Islam. They are among the first tenets of Islam that are taught to young people growing up in the Muslim tradition.

Performing these duties sincerely, out of love for God, assures the believer of a place in paradise. These are every Muslim's personal as well as communal obligations, and are taken as an expression of faith and devotion.

Declaration of Faith (shahadah)

The first pillar of Islam is *shahadah*, or "declaration of faith." Shahadah contains two declarations:

First: "I bear witness that there is no god but God."

Second: "I bear witness that Muhammad is the Messenger of God."

The first declaration is an affirmation of God's oneness and is the primary principle of monotheism, which is shared with Judaism and Christianity. According to Islam, belief in the oneness of God and submission to God's will (i.e., Islam) is the primordial state of faith in which every child is born (in previous chapters we referred to this stage as *fitrah*). The second declaration is the affirmation of acceptance of Muhammad as the last messenger (*rasul*) of God.

Throughout Islamic history, declaration of these two principles has been the primary precondition of accepting Islam as one's religion. Non-Muslims who are inclined toward converting to Islam need to recite these declarations aloud in order to be accepted into the community of Muslims as a fellow believer. Although public declaration of these principles officially protects a person's rights as a Muslim, it will not lead to salvation if these concepts are not sincerely internalized. Shahadah has to be supported by deep personal faith (*iman*) and righteous act (*ihsan*).

Prayer (salat)

The second pillar of Islam is *salat*, or "prayers." We covered this pillar in Chapter 5, when we discussed the concept of worship in Islam.

Almsgiving (zakat)

The third pillar of Islam is *zakat*, or "almsgiving." Zakat literally means to purify or increase; it is believed that when one renders zakat, his or her remaining property is purified. Zakat is an obligatory annual taxation paid by adult Muslims for the good of their community. It amounts to 2.5 percent of one's accumulated wealth, including savings earned through business transactions, inheritance, or any other sources. It is given at the end of each year to help the poor and to improve the community. During the early centuries of Islam's existence, when governments functioned within the context of religion, the revenue earned by collected zakat was kept in a treasury house. The money then was used to satisfy the collective needs of the society, such as public education, civic projects, public security, protection of orphans and the dispossessed, and to help travelers in need and released war captives, or for other similar needs (Q. 9:60).

Today, Muslims are scattered in many different countries in which laws are based on Western secular principles rather than *shari'ah* (Islamic law). In the majority of these countries, governments have their own taxation programs, part of the revenues of which are used for the common good, so rendering zakat would place an extra financial burden upon many Muslims. Therefore, this obligatory pillar of Islam has become mostly voluntarily for Muslims in such situations. Believers who want to pay their zakat either find their own needy recipients or render it through religious and charitable organizations.

In addition to the obligatory zakat, a form of voluntary almsgiving known as *sadaqah* (charity) is also encouraged by the Qur'an. The Qur'an considers sadaqah similar to a loan given to God: "Who will give a generous loan to God? He will pay him back tenfold and he will receive a rich reward" (Q. 57:11).

Fasting (saum)

Saum, or "fasting," is the fourth pillar of Islam. Every year, during the entire month of *Ramadan*, which is the ninth month of the Islamic lunar calendar, adult Muslims are obligated to fast from dawn to dusk. Fasting involves abstinence from food, drink, medicine, smoking, sex, and any other sensual pleasure. Nothing external can enter the body through the mouth, injection, or other means. The fast is broken after sunset prayers, and those who fasted the whole day are then permitted to eat, drink, and enjoy marital relations if they so desire.

During Ramadan, families generally awake and eat just before dawn so that their bodies will have sufficient nutritional strength to get through a day of fasting. Since the Islamic calendar is lunar-based, the month of Ramadan changes within the seasons as time progresses. When it occurs in summer, fasting becomes more difficult during the long and hot days, especially for Muslims who live in arid regions of the Middle East and Africa.

Fasting is not required for everyone. Children, the elderly, the infirm, travelers, and pregnant and menstruating women are exempted from fasting. However, adults who miss days of fasting for any reason are required to make up for the missed days whenever they can. Every religion has practitioners who try to escape the more difficult observances, and Islam is no exception: Some procrastinating Muslims schedule their vacations for Ramadan in order to—at least temporarily—escape fasting. If they fail to make up every day of fasting that they missed, however, they postpone the fulfillment of this obligation and accrue a spiritual deficit with God.

The Qur'an prescribes fasting during the month of Ramadan:

> O believers, fasting is prescribed to you as it was upon those before you, so that you might (learn) self-restraint. Fast a fixed number of days, but if any one among you is ill or on a journey, let him fast a similar number of days later, and for those who cannot endure it, it can be expiated by the feeding of a poor man. He that does good of his own accord shall be rewarded, but to fast is better for you if you knew. In the month of Ramadan the Qur'an was revealed, a book of guidance with signs of guidance distinguishing right from wrong. Therefore, whoever of you is present [in his home], in that month let him fast. But he who is ill or on a journey shall fast a similar number of days later, as God wishes you well-being and not hardship. He desires you to fast the whole month so that you may glorify Him and render thanks to Him for giving you His guidance (Q. 2:183–185).

Because the Qur'an was revealed to Muhammad during the month of Ramadan, this is considered a holy time in the Islamic year. During this sacred month, believers often reflect upon their spiritual and ethical lives, perform their missed prayers, and recite the Qur'an. Also, fasting allows the faithful to experience the hardship of being deprived of food and water, so they develop better sympathy for the poor and dispossessed, who may not have the luxuries, or even the basic necessities, of life.

Ramadan is a joyous month, especially throughout Arab countries, and families often gather in each other's homes or congregate in mosques and other religious places. In the evenings, restaurants and shops are crowded with people and one can hear the sound of music being played throughout the city.

Pilgrimage to Mecca (Hajj)

The fifth and final pillar of Islam is the *hajj*, or pilgrimage to Mecca. Hajj is a requirement for all Muslims who have the physical, mental, and financial ability to make the journey. If a person is financially able but physically unable to make the trip, he or she can finance the trip of another person who is physically able but financially unable, and thus fulfill this religious obligation. The main purpose of hajj is to provide Muslims from all walks of life and from various parts of the world with an opportunity to gather in one place and experience the unity of Islamic community (*ummah*) both spiritually and socially. The pilgrimage is performed during the lunar month of *Dhul Hijjah*, the twelfth month of the Islamic calendar.

The destination for hajj is the Kaaba, the house of God in Mecca, in present-day Saudi Arabia. According to Islamic tradition, this fifteen-meter-high cubic structure was originally built by Abraham and his son Ishmael and was dedicated to the worship of the one God (Q. 22:25–27). It is a symbol of monotheism and an emblem linking Muhammad to earlier prophets and Islam to earlier monotheistic religions. At the time of Muhammad, pilgrimage to the Kaaba was an ancient pagan rite; however, after conquering the city of Mecca, Muhammad once again dedicated the house to the worship of the one God. Today's rituals of hajj are a reenactment of the experiences of Abraham, the father of monotheism and forefather of the Arabs, and of his Egyptian wife Hagar. They also provide an opportunity for remembering the life and times of Muhammad and the challenge he faced in setting out to make Islam a universal religion.

The pilgrimage is an experience that a Muslim never forgets. It is an opportunity to be among millions of Muslims from all racial, linguistic, and ethnic backgrounds. Due to the ever-increasing ease of modern transportation, each year, more than 2 million Muslims make the pilgrimage during the required days. They come from all over the world.

Before reaching the sacred city of Mecca, male pilgrims exchange their regular clothes for a two-piece white seamless garment that symbolizes the shrouds in which people are wrapped for burial. This is considered a way to reunite with their creator God. In their white clean garment, they enter the ritually pure and consecrated state known as *ihram*. Women can wear either a white garment that covers the entire body and head or they may simply choose clean and modest clothing. When in Mecca and in the state of ihram, pilgrims abstain from sexual relations, from shaving their beards or cutting any bodily hair, from wearing perfume or expensive jewelry, and from hunting animals or cutting trees.

The rituals of hajj include circumambulation (*tawaf*) of the Kaaba in a counterclockwise direction, and running between the two hills of al-Safa and al-Marwa. According to Islamic tradition, when Abraham left Hagar, his Egyptian wife, and their son, Ishmael, in the deserts of Mecca as God commanded him to, Hagar ran worriedly between these two hills to find water for her thirsty infant son, Ishmael. After the seventh lap, by God's command, water gushed out from where the thirsty Ishmael lay kicking the ground. The spot from which that water emerged is known as the well of Zamzam today. The water of Zamzam is considered holy, so upon their return home, pilgrims bring with them containers of Zamzam water as blessed gifts for their family and friends.

The formal pilgrimage begins on the eighth day of the month Dhul Hijjah when the pilgrims go to Mina, east of Mecca, to stand in the plain of 'Arafat, which contains the Mount of Mercy. On the ninth of Dhul Hijjah, pilgrims stand on this plain from noon until dark in *wuquf*, or "the Standing State." This is the pinnacle of the whole ritual because this symbolizes the Last Day, when all humanity will stand before God, awaiting his judgment. These are the hours when pilgrims contemplate and reflect upon their lives and ask forgiveness through their prayers.

Standing on the plain of 'Arafat is also significant because, according to Islamic tradition, it is the place where Adam and Eve stood after their expulsion from paradise, where Abraham and his son Ishmael performed the first pilgrimage, and where Muhammad gave his final sermon, which announced the last revelation from God and affirmed the completion of Islam as a religion for all of humankind.

On the tenth day of Dhul Hijjah, the pilgrimage officially reaches its end and the four-day festival of sacrifice starts. This festival is a commemoration of Abraham's sacrifice of an animal after God showed his mercy by sparing his son Ishmael, who was supposed to have been sacrificed by divine command. (Jews and Christians believe Abraham was told to sacrifice his other son, Isaac.) In thankfulness to God for his generosity and benevolence, Muslims sacrifice an animal such as a sheep, goat, cattle, or camel and share the meat with the poor.

After the formal pilgrimage is completed, many Muslims visit the tomb of Muhammad and the shrine of his mosque, the first Muslim mosque, in Medina. Upon their return home, pilgrims acquire the title of *hajji*, meaning "one who has completed the hajj." Muslims attain some prestige by fulfilling the demanding requirements of hajj, and they are proud to attach the title of hajji to their names.

The experience of hajj usually has a profound impact upon the life of the believer. Perhaps the life of Malcolm X, the well-known African-American Muslim and militant civil rights leader exemplifies this transformation. Prior to his trip to Mecca, Malcolm X preached racism in the name of Islam and called whites the "blue-eyed devil." While in Mecca, however, he observed many devoted white Muslims standing shoulder to shoulder with him, and people of all other races doing the pilgrimage. The spiritual impact of hajj and the egalitarian participation of all pilgrims completely changed Malcolm X. Upon his return to the United States, he began to preach the all-inclusive universal nature of Islam, which does not recognize ethnic differences or the superiority of one race over another.

THE ISLAMIC COMMUNITY (*UMMAH*)

From childhood, Muslims learn that belief unsupported by right behavior is almost without value, and that they need to enact their belief in regular practice. Islam envisions a community based upon morality and justice, and it is the duty of each Muslim to do his or her part to attain such a just and moral community. The Qur'an states, "You are the best community evolved for humankind by enjoining what is right and forbidding what is wrong . . ." (Q. 3:110). This passage has been interpreted by many Muslims as a command to justify social, political, and moral activism within their own communities. Thus, spreading God's rule becomes an individual as well as community obligation.

Governments such as those of Iran and Saudi Arabia that try to control the moral behavior of their populations contend that the activities of their so-called "moral police" are upholding Islam's divine command to promote good and prevent evil. In this imperfect world, when fallible or misguided or opportunistic people are placed in charge of implementing the word of God, the simple notion of proscribing behavior deemed evil quickly becomes the subjective harassment of lawful and even devout citizens. Such bands of government-sanctioned religious vigilantes are not unlike the punitive religious zealots of early American history. Such groups often provoke hostility toward religious observance, the opposite of their stated reason for existing.

The Qur'an emphasizes the equality of humankind in the sight of God: "O humankind, We have created you from a male and a female, and made you into nations and tribes, that you might know one another. The noblest of you in God's sight is the most righteous among you. God is the All-knowing and the Wise" (Q. 49:13). Islam replaced kinship status with right conduct as the arbiter of nobility. Therefore, the Muslim community overall is more strongly bonded by common belief than by kinship. This basic bond of the early Islamic community matured into the concept of an *ummah*, or "nation," that embraces the entire worldwide Islamic community.

The cornerstones of the Islamic community are justice and

equality: "O believers, feel your duties to God and bear true witness. Do not allow your hatred for other men to turn you away from justice. Deal justly, that is nearer to true piety. Be aware of God, God is cognizant of all your actions" (Q. 5:8). Muhammad himself was a major reformer of his time. His social reform was based upon individual transformation and obligations as well as collective moral and social responsibility. The Qur'an envisions a sense of community based upon equality, justice, fairness, brotherhood, mercy, compassion, solidarity, and free will for all its participants. Striving for this was the lifelong effort of the prophet Muhammad. In Islam, community leaders are responsible for the application of the principles of Islam, and they are held accountable to God and to their people for the quality of their performance. A genuine Islamic community is governed by the Islamic law, or *shari'ah*.

ISLAMIC LAW (*SHARI'AH*)

Shari'ah literally means "a path to a source of water," and the term is understood to refer to the divinely mandated path of Islam, which, if rightly followed, will lead the Muslim community to salvation in this life and after death. Like Judaism, Islam emphasizes observance of law over theology and orthodoxy, and the Islamic notion of shari'ah can be compared with the Torah (i.e., law or instructions) that governs Jewish life and transactions. Shari'ah contains laws that are based mainly upon the teachings of the Qur'an and the example of the prophet Muhammad. Shari'ah is also a source of moral guidance. In Islam, there is no separation between legality and morality, because of the absoluteness of God's sovereignty. Therefore, God's guidance through his revelations and the examples of his prophets is the main source for the best way to conduct everyday life, including moral, legal, social, and political affairs.

As Islam spread throughout the world, a need grew for a more uniform shari'ah, so scholars and jurists worked hard to develop a comprehensive law applicable to different parts of the

Islamic Empire. Most of the body of Islamic law was written during the early centuries of the Abbasid Empire, a dynasty that reigned from 750 to 1258. The four early scholars who were instrumental in developing the shari'ah were Abu Hanifa (d. 767), the founder of the Hanafi school of law in Baghdad; Malik ibn Anas (d. 796), who was a judge in Medina and founded the Maleki school; Muhammad al-Shafii (d. 819), who was a disciple of Malik ibn Anas and founded the Shafii school; and Ahmad ibn Hanbal (d. 855), who founded the Hanbali school. The Hanafi school allowed more personal reasoning (*ijtihad*) than the other three did. All four schools, however, recognize the systems of the others as equally orthodox. The Hanbali school is the strictest in its interpretation of the Qur'an and ahadith. It was actually established as a reaction to what ibn Hanbal considered speculative innovations by the other three schools. The school of law most popular among Shiites is the Ja'fari school, which was founded by the sixth Shiite imam, Ja'far al-Sadiiq (d. 765).

Of all these scholars, al-Shafii is the one considered the father of Islamic jurisprudence. Al-Shafii recognized four sources of Islamic law, which are still recognized today. They are:

1. the Qur'an,

2. the sunnah (examples and teachings of the Prophet),

3. qiyas: analogical reasoning or deduction, and

4. ijma: consensus of the community.

The first two are divinely inspired and, as such, are considered the most important sources of law. Qiyas is analogical reasoning with reference to the Qur'an and Sunnah. For example, juridical investigators might try to determine whether women are legally allowed to drive (in Saudi Arabia, for example, women are not permitted to drive). First, they would examine the Qur'an, but, since it was revealed in the seventh century, it contains no references to automobiles or driving. Next, they would resort to a secondary source, the sunnah of the Prophet, but again, the collection of narrations about the Prophet's sunnah closed in the ninth century, and likewise contain no references to either cars or driving. Here, qiyas comes to the rescue. The investigators might construct an analogy based upon the general function of vehicles (such as carts) and extrapolate that to include modern vehicles. The function of a car is to transfer people from one place to another, and as such, replaces horses, camels, carriages, and other modes of transportation. The next and necessary question would be to inquire if there existed any laws that prevented women from riding such animals or operating such transports. The answer, of course, is no. Thus, by analogy and the use of the qiyas element of shari'ah, the investigators would conclude that women are indeed allowed to drive automobiles.

FEMALE CIRCUMCISION

Although the practice of circumcision has no basis in the Qur'an, according to Muhammad, "circumcision is a law for men and a preservation of honor for women," and it remains an important obligation for some Muslims. These Muslims see circumcision as an introduction into and sign of belonging to their religion. Male circumcision is performed primarily for cleanliness and is officially embraced by the Islamic community. Female circumcision, however, is more of a cultural than a religious practice, and it has come under scrutiny because many people, both inside and outside the Muslim community, see it as a form of mutilation and a violation of women's rights. In this procedure, the main goal is to curb the woman's sexual desire, and depending upon the customs of those performing the circumcision, part or, in some instances, all of the female genitalia is removed. This cultural tradition is now practiced almost exclusively in Islamic Africa and among some non-Muslim populations of sub-Saharan Africa. It can result in hemorrhaging, infection, chronic pain, infertility, and death in extreme cases. In recent decades, organizations such as the United Nations, the World Health Organization, and Amnesty International have begun campaigns against this practice, although there is little indication of its decline.

7

Cultural Expressions

One of the hallmarks of civilized man is knowledge of the past—[including] the past of others with whom one's own culture has had repeated and fruitful contact; or the past of any group that has contributed to the ascent of man. The Arabs fit profoundly into both of the latter two categories. But in the West the Arabs are not well known. Victims of ignorance as well as misinformation, they and their culture have often been stigmatized from afar.

—John Hayes, *The Genius of Arab Civilization: Source of the Renaissance*

MULTICULTURAL CIVILIZATION

One of the greatest achievements of Islam during its golden age (the ninth to thirteenth centuries) was uniting the great economic regions of the Mediterranean basin and Asia, and creating a peaceful setting for the mingling of people from a variety of cultural backgrounds. The political stability achieved by powerful Muslim rulers secured the major international roads, which in turn allowed an incredible volume of trade throughout the Islamic Empire. Along with agriculture and industry, trade (both regional and international) was a major source of income for the Islamic state. Trade brought material prosperity, especially to urban areas, and as is always the case, allowed for a free flow of ideas and information that helped knowledge flourish. Trade brought an opportunity for culturally diverse peoples to meet and exchange ideas and discuss religion, art, science, and all kinds of topics relevant to everyday life. Some of the conquered peoples of the Islamic Empire had inherited rich and sophisticated cultures and civilizations from their ancestors. The new empire, therefore, became a conglomeration of Semitic, Hellenistic (Greek), Spanish, Iranian, and Indian cultures; it was truly multinational in nature. The knowledge acquired from all these contacts became the backbone of Islamic civilization in the Middle Ages.

Besides political stability, trade, and material prosperity, there were other factors that also contributed to the advancement of Islamic science, technology, art, architecture, jurisprudence, and philosophy. These included an inherent thirst for knowledge within the Islamic worldview, Muslim rulers' encouragement and patronage, and a wealth of information available through access to the rich heritage of ancient civilizations.

Both the Qur'an and the Prophet stressed the value of knowledge and education. The Qur'an calls believers to look at the universe as an open book and to study its patterns. This religious instruction made Muslim scholars particularly interested in natural science, and they left a substantial record of their observations (Q. 20:114). Muhammad also constantly emphasized the value of education and the search for knowledge. He is known for statements such as: "Searching for knowledge is a religious duty of any Muslim man and Muslim woman"; "Seek knowledge from cradle to grave"; "Seek knowledge even if it will take you to China" (China being considered the farthest place from Arabia in his time); and "The reward for studying is the same as the reward for fasting and the reward for teaching is the same as the reward for prayers." Encouragement from religious sources and authorities had a great impact on Muslims' determination on striving for knowledge.

Many Muslim rulers, both out of piety and self-desire, promoted knowledge during their reigns by building educational institutions and helping promising scholars through generous grants and scholarships. Major rulers made supporting scientists and engineers a priority. The rulers of smaller states later adopted this policy as well. Financial assistance was given to scientists to allow them to devote all their time to study and research. Scientists who worked for established educational institutions were paid a regular salary and granted pensions. Some caliphs, such as al-Mu'tadid (d. 902), set aside places for scholars to teach and live within their own palaces.

There was a wealth of knowledge left from Greek, Persian, and other earlier sophisticated civilizations that was ready to be tapped. There was a large body of literature in Syriac, Greek, Latin, Persian, and Sanskrit languages, which could be useful to scholars. For example, because of Egypt's pre-Islamic contact with Greece, Egypt had become a conduit for the development and spread of Greek culture through the Mediterranean region. Trade relations with Greece gave Egyptian scientists knowledge of Greek science and philosophy. So, when Egypt became part of the Islamic Empire in 641, Muslims, too, began to utilize Greek-developed science and philosophy.

The great heritage of knowledge available in science, technology, the humanities, and government administration was drawn into the emerging Islamic civilization. There was, for instance, a large body of literature available in the Pahlawi language of

Persia dealing with the art of government, office administration, and royal etiquette. Some of the best indirect advice to rulers came from a Persian book of literature called *Kalilah wa Dimnah*, a brilliant work that communicates its message to the reader thorough moralistic fables of animal life in a way that might remind modern readers of George Orwell's celebrated book *Animal Farm*.

There was also available technical literature tied to various fields, ranging from military tactics to agriculture and irrigation. Perhaps the most useful knowledge available was in the disciplines of medicine, astronomy, and mathematics, which were brought to scholars through the Jundishapur educational center, a sophisticated facility in southern Persia that included large and impressive libraries.

Greek culture had perhaps the greatest impact on the development of Islamic civilization, particularly in the field of philosophy. Islamic culture followed the Greek emphasis on reason, logic, and the laws of nature. Muslim intellectuals wanted to understand concepts such as God and revelation through reason. They wanted to equip themselves with reasonable arguments to help them prove the absolute oneness of God and the concept of transcendence that was so important to them, as well as to argue against any anthropomorphism presented by other religions.

They wanted to know if the attributes of God outlined in the Qur'an actually identify God as a being with a body like that of a human or are such descriptions merely metaphorical? Was the concept of the Trinity in Christianity a form of polytheism or it was another legitimate metaphorical way of understanding God? Was the Qur'an (the last revelation of God, as Muslims perceived it) eternal or created? Did God predetermine the destinies of human beings or could people change the direction of their own fate? If God is truly compassionate about his favorite creature, the human being, then why did he create Satan to tempt humans?

Influenced by Greek thinkers such as Socrates, Plato, and

Aristotle, some Muslim intellectuals devoted their whole careers to writing about the interaction between faith and reason. Some Muslim scholars found the relationship between humans and God as dictated by Islamic law and explained by the *'ulama* (learned men) too rigid, too formal, and too impersonal for their taste. On the other hand, they did not want to rationalize God or follow him based on blind faith; rather, they wanted to experience God within their hearts. The people who followed this line of reasoning became known as Sufis.

EXPRESSION OF GOD THROUGH LOVE: THE SUFI PATH *(TARIQAH)*

> *O Lord,*
> *If I worship You*
> *From fear of Hell, burn me in Hell.*
> *O Lord,*
> *If I worship You*
> *From hope of Paradise, bar me from its gates.*
> *But if I worship You for Yourself alone*
> *Then grace me forever the splendor of Your Face.*[4]

This lovely poem by Rabi'ah (d. 801) illustrates the essence of Sufism: unconditional love.

An anecdote further explains Sufi beliefs: A flute-playing slave child was gradually introduced to teachings of Islam. Her master noticed her exceptional spiritual devotion and realized that she had already chosen her real master (God). So, he set her free.

That slave child was Rabi'ah. She was passionate about her love for God and demonstrated her admiration for her creator in enchanting poetry. Though she was a very attractive woman who received many offers of marriage, she refused them all and instead chose a life of asceticism, remaining unwed for the rest of her life. When asked about her decision to reject married life, she responded that her heart was so fully devoted to God that she could not possibly share it with any other being. Her simple life and joyful love for God attracted many followers for whom she served as an example and guide. Her life and poetry greatly influenced the development of a passion-oriented Sufism.

Sufism is the compassionate heart of Islam. It provides the necessary nourishment for the body and is also the spirit that can see beyond the physical limitations of the body. In searching for truth, it can detach itself from its confinement and fly above it with bird's-eye vision, a holistic view of God and the universe that is not possible from within the confinement of the body. The observant spirit becomes a bridge between the body and the outside world and acts as a peacemaker. The loving heart avoids rigidity and conflicts and solicits instead cooperation, inclusiveness, and understanding. Perhaps no one can better explain the heart of a Sufi than the great Sufi Ibn al-Arabi (d. 1240):

> *O Marvel! a garden amidst the flames.*
> *My heart has become capable of every form:*
> *it is a pasture for gazelles and a convent for Christian monks,*
> *and a temple for idols and the pilgrim's Kaaba,*
> *and the tables of the Torah and the book of the Qur'an.*
> *I follow the religion of Love: whatever way Love's camels take,*
> *that is my religion and my faith.*[5]

Ibn al-Arabi, a great Sufi poet and scholar, developed the doctrine of "The Unity of Being." In it, he states that, since all creation is a manifestation of the transcendent God, all forms of creation are, in essence, identical to him. Ibn al-Arabi continued by saying that, although God is necessary for humanity to exist, it may also be true that humanity is necessary for God to be manifested. He defended his doctrine by referring to a hadith that conveyed a message from God that declared: "I was a hidden treasure and wanted to be known, thus I created the world that I might be known."[6] This verse does not exist in the Qur'an; it is one of Muhammad's own inspirations by God; but there are other verses in the Qur'an that contain similar messages: "The seven heavens, the earth, and all who dwell in them give glory to him. All creatures celebrate his praises. Yet you cannot understand their praises. Forbearing is he and forgiving" (Q. 17:44, 51:56).

Ibn al-Arabi's doctrine, that the universe is a reflection of God, established a dialogue among Muslim scholars. His views were attractive to Sufis and many followed his lead.

Like Ibn al-Arabi, other Sufis were inspired by the life of the prophet Muhammad and made him their prototype. Sufis understood Muhammad as a man who passed no one without a smile on his face. For Sufis, Muhammad's generosity and compassion were his most important qualities to emulate. Sufis often recall an incident related to the Prophet that happened during the early years of Islam when the pagans of Mecca were constantly harassing Muhammad. One day, as Muhammad was walking along his usual path, he was surprised when a man who usually threw garbage on his head was not around to bother him. Muhammad asked after the man and was informed that the man was sick. Muhammad visited the ailing man at his house. The man was stunned that Muhammad was paying him a visit, despite the way he had treated the Prophet in the past. Muhammad greeted him with smile, expressed his worries about the man's condition, and wished him good health. The man was so moved by Muhammad's generosity and kindness that he decided to accept Muhammad's message of Islam. For Sufis, this example of Muhammad's compassion is a path to God.

Sufism is called *tasawwuf* in Arabic, meaning "purification." The name refers to the fact that the Sufi is known as someone who purifies his or her mind and body. Sufis are also called *faqir* ("poor") or *darwish*, a Persian term meaning "poor" or "mendicant." According to popular tradition, the term *Sufi* is derived from the Arabic term *suf*, meaning "wool," which refers to a simple woolen garment worn by Sufi mystics. The attire of Sufis who symbolically shun the material world contrasts sharply with the rich apparel of those who are attached to worldly things. Since the selection of the clothing that one wears is, to some degree, an ego-oriented process, by wearing simple dress, Sufis plainly express their lack of egoism. In the eyes of Sufis, the biggest hurdle standing in the way of reaching God is the ego. To them, ego is like a hernia; the more it swells, the more

FROM THE
ISLAMIC
TRADITION

A view of *Haram* (*al-Masjid al-Haram*) where the *Kaaba* is located. Every year, more than 2 million faithful Muslims from all over the world visit this holiest Muslim site in Mecca, Saudi Arabia, during the month of *Hajj* (*Dhul Hijjah.*)

Carpets and rugs cover the floors of mosques, particularly the praying sanctuaries. This picture depicts a prayer rug with *mihrab* motif.

Although the majority of pilgrims to Mecca these days come via airplane, in earlier times, the pilgrimage was often made on foot or on animals' backs. This painting depicts a group of nineteenth-century pilgrims en route to Mecca.

The Dome of the Rock is one the holiest Muslim shrines. It was from here that the prophet Muhammad, according to Islamic tradition, ascended to heaven to meet with God.

This image from the Dome of the Rock illustrates the use of calligraphy and geometric design. Because illustration of human and animal images is forbidden in Islamic mosques, Muslim artists have traditionally made creative use of calligraphy and geometric and flowery designs in Islamic architecture.

This view of the *Jameh* Mosque in Isfahan, Iran, highlights the mosaic decoration of the interior dome.

This picture depicts the Third Rightly Guided caliph, 'Uthman. During the reign of 'Uthman (644–656) the Qur'an (as we know it today) was written in its final form.

it hurts. The great Sufi Abu Saeed Abil Kheir expresses his views on the containment of ego and the expression of generosity as a necessary path to God:

> Suppose you can recite a thousand holy verses from memory. What are you going to do with your ego self, the true mark of the heretic? Every time your head touches the ground in prayers, remember, this was to teach you to put down that load of ego which bars you from entering the chamber of the Beloved.
>
> To your mind feed understanding, to your heart, tolerance and compassion. The simpler your life, the more meaningful. The less you desire of the world, the more room you will have in it to fill with the Beloved.
>
> The best use of your tongue is to repeat the Beloved's Name in devotion. The best prayers are those in the solitude of the night. The shortest way to the Friend is through selfless service and generosity to His creatures.[7]

Historically speaking, Sufism was also a social reaction to the moral laxity, worldliness, and extravagance of the Umayyad caliphs who took over the leadership of Islamic state after the death of Muhammad and his immediate successors. Many Muslims saw a clear deviation from the egalitarian teachings of Islam in the selfish leadership of the Umayyad caliphs. The alienation from the *ummah* (Islamic community) that began in the Umayyads' time continued under the Abbasid caliphs, and Sufis again took an issue with the style in which the ummah was governed. One of the early critics of caliphs' excesses was the Sufi Master Hassan al-Basri (d. 728), who had many students, including the poet Rabi'ah. He considered the material world the "lower world," a trap for those who seek spiritual liberation. The Sufis who followed Hassan al-Basri shared his views warned their followers against the temptations of money, fame, and power.

The path that Sufis choose to reach God is known as *tariqah*. Like the term *shari'ah*, it literally means "a path." However, Sufis consider shari'ah an external path and tariqah the internal path to God. Sufis believe both paths are needed in order to reach God: The external path based on shari'ah defines individual and community rights and duties, while the internal way based on tariqah is a path that helps develop discipline toward God. Between these external and internal dimensions of Islam, Muslims enjoy a balanced and spiritual life.

Though al-Basri was among the early *'ulama* (the hadith scholars, jurists, and theologians), he saw it as his religious duty to speak out against what he saw as the wasteful life of the political elite. In the eyes of Sufis, those members of the 'ulama who observed the misbehavior of political and social rulers and remained indifferent were hypocrites. The desire to correct the ills of society encouraged some popular Sufi masters to turn to politics and actively work for the public. In their view, serving their fellow human beings was the same as serving God, since the universe—including humanity—is a reflection of God.

The mainstream or traditional 'ulama and the Sufis did not always acknowledge each other. Some 'ulama saw the religious practice of Sufis as too liberal and, in some cases, blasphemous. They were sometimes hostile to Sufis and used their political power against them. For example, when Sufi thinker Mansour al-Hallaj, in manifesting his union with God, declared, "I am the Truth," some of the more fanatic 'ulama took his statement as a statement of polytheism and labeled him an apostate and heretic. Based on their advice, al-Hallaj was brutally executed in Baghdad in 922. According to Mansour al-Hallaj's devout students, he died smiling and heralding the approach of his meeting with God. This can clearly be depicted from his poetic words at the time of his death:

> *I am He whom I love, and He whom I love is I,*
> *We are two spirits dwelling in one body.*
> *If thou seest me, thou seest Him,*
> *And if thou seest Him, thou seest us both.*[8]

The gap between Sufis and the stern religious leaders continued to grow over time, and each side was critical of the other. Sufis wanted to move beyond the religious formalities propagated by the 'ulama and criticized the legal moral Islam imposed on people by the often hypocritical 'ulama who aligned themselves with the government. Although some 'ulama were moderate in their approach to the Sufis (some 'ulama were even Sufis themselves), the majority considered Sufis a threat to their power and dismissed Sufi doctrines as heretical deviations from orthodox Islam. This is the view presently held by the Wahabbis in modern Saudi Arabia.

The tension between Sufis and 'ulama was reduced significantly when one of the most celebrated scholars among the 'ulama, Abu Hamid al-Ghazali (d. 1111) became a Sufi. Al-Ghazali wrote about his transition in his autobiography: "I probed the motives of my teaching and found that, in place of being sincerely consecrated to God, it was only actuated by a vain desire of honor and reputation."[9] Disappointed with his lack of sincerity and his fall for worldly temptations, he left his very highly respected position and chose to live as a Sufi. He traveled to different regions, met with scholars and ascetics from all walks of life, and wrote about his spiritual metamorphosis in his masterpiece, *Revivification of the Religious Science*, one of the greatest works of all time for seekers of God and students of religion.

According to a saying of the Prophet, "there are as many paths to God as there are children of Adam." So today, there are many Sufis with many different paths. The Sufi spiritual master defines his path (*tariqah*) and, after his death, one of his protégés will take over the responsibility, and then, he, too, will eventually pass it on to the next qualified person.

The Sufi master is usually referred to as *Shaykh* (*pir* in Persian), meaning "master." Usually, the Sufi master tries to establish a line of spiritual guides for his pupils, which is traceable all the way to the prophet Muhammad or his cousin 'Ali. Sufis gather in a place called *zawiyyah* or *khanqah*, both kinds of Sufi hospices. Al-Ghazali established one of the first official Sufi centers. Some well-established Sufi orders have a khanqah where the master and his family reside, along with rooms set aside for disciples. Followers are usually formally initiated after a certain period of time and then become regular members. Centers are usually built with the income from pious endowments. The larger centers have sleeping rooms and soup kitchens for the poor. Many of the great Sufis were also great scientists and studied under accomplished masters in educational institutions.

Sufi gatherings are marked by *dhikr* (*zikr*), or remembrance of God in the form of chanting. The chants are usually verses from the Qur'an or pieces of uplifting religious poetry. Some Sufi orders, such as the Whirling Dervishes, who are inspired by the famous Persian poet and philosopher Jalal al-Di Rumi (d. 1273), perform a ritual turning dance along with their dhikr.

EDUCATIONAL INSTITUTIONS

Many scientific academies, schools, libraries, and observatories were established during the golden age of Islamic civilization. One of the most important scientific centers was the Bayt al-Hikmah (House of Wisdom) in Baghdad, built by the Abbasid caliph al-Ma'mun in 820. This academy was an improvement over the Khizanat al-Hikma (Library of Wisdom) established by Ma'mun's father Harun al-Rashid in 809. A major task of the Bayt al-Hikma was to translate works of science and humanities from Greek, Latin, Syriac, Pahlavi (Persian), and Sanskrit (Indian) into Arabic, so they could be used by Muslim scholars. The academy included a staff of eminent scientists and translators and was known for publishing accurate and reliable editions; it also included many experienced copyists and bookbinders.

Scientists and translators worked in a tolerant atmosphere where people from many nationalities and religions cooperated. For example, the academy was supervised by the well-known Nestorian Christian Hunain ibn Ishaq, and included staff members from other ethnic and religious backgrounds as well.

By the eleventh century, numerous books had already been translated by the academy, including the works of eighty Greek thinkers—scholars such as Aristotle, Plato, Galen, and Euclid. The topics of translated works included philosophy, literature, religion, government, medicine, mathematics, physics, astronomy, astrology, alchemy, and even magic. In addition to translation, the academy staff was involved in independent scientific research and experiments.

Science Centers

Scholars such as the Banu Musa brothers made significant progress in advancing the field of astronomy. There were two observatory centers attached to the academy for practical experiments. Observatories carried out both research and teaching. The most important Muslim observatory was the one in Maraghah in northwestern Iran, where Naser al-Din Tusi, the well-known astronomer and mathematician, worked. Many international scientists cooperated on major projects in this institution. Some other later Muslim observatories, such as Ulugh Beg in Samarqand and Taqi al-Din in Istanbul, served as models for early European observatories such as that built by astronomer Tycho Brahe on the island of Hven in the Sont near Copenhagen (it closed down in 1597).

Other Muslim rulers also adopted the policy of implementing science by building scientific centers. For example, in 998, Fatamid ruler al-Hakim established the Dar al-Ilm (Abode of Science) inside his huge palace in Cairo. The facility contained a library and reading room, and served as a meeting place for religious scholars, jurists, linguists, physicians, astronomers, and mathematicians. The center was directed by a well-known scholar who held regular seminars dealing with different scientific topics and invited specialists from various parts of the world to share their findings with their fellow scientists. Lectures were open to the public and the interested audience was provided with ink, pens, and paper for note-taking.[10]

Libraries and Educational Facilities

In addition to major centers, there were many smaller places of learning established by public funds. Libraries were very popular. All major mosques had their own libraries. Usually, people donated books to these libraries. It was also customary for notable people with substantial financial means to build mosques and libraries.

During the hours between official prayers, religious or even secular teachers held classes at mosques and any interested students participated. A widespread desire for education led to the creation of *madrasahs* (schools) near or attached to major mosques where students could receive formal religious training or other types of education. Madrasahs became major institutions that still survive in many traditional Muslim cities. A large number of the Afghan Taliban were trained in madrasahs in the city of Peshawar, near Pakistan's border with Afghanistan.

Some madrasahs expanded and became universities. Among the early Islamic universities were the al-Azhar in Cairo, Egypt; Zaytuniya in Tunis, Tunisia; and Qarawiyyin in Fez, Morocco. Many of the medical schools associated with these universities had their own hospitals. These institutions taught medicine, had research facilities, and required students to work with actual patients. Al-Azhar, established in Cairo in 969, remains a well-rounded university in Cairo and is the oldest surviving university in the world. It was established long before the first universities emerged in Europe, starting in the eleventh century. (A university opened in Bologna around 1088, followed by one in Paris around 1155.)

GROWTH AND DEVELOPMENT OF ISLAMIC SCIENCE

The great Islamic thinkers of the golden age were true Renaissance men (although they preceded the coining of the term by several centuries). They were philosophers, theologians, physicians, mathematicians, and poets, and they were very skillful in all the fields at which they tried their hand. Of course, one reason for this is the requirements of the time. During the Islamic golden age, disciplinary divisions were not established as they are today. Scholars were known for the breadth of their knowledge, and did not usually specialize in a particular science. Also, when scholars were hired by a caliph or other ruler to work on a task, they often had to accept the offer, regardless of whether they were trained in the discipline required, due to financial needs, respect, or simply fear of the leader involved. In his book *Introduction to History of Science*, George Sarton, in explaining the great contribution of Muslim scholars to the development of science, makes references to some of these towering figures:

> It will suffice here to evoke a few glorious names without contemporary equivalents in the West: Jabir ibn Haiyan, al-Kindi, al-Khwarizmi, al-Fargani, al-Razi, Thabit ibn Qurra, al-Battani, Hunain ibn Ishaq, al-Farabi, Ibrahim ibn Sinan, al-Masudi, al-Tabari, Abul Wafa, 'Ali ibn Abbas, Abul Qasim, Ibn al-Jazzar, al-Biruni, Ibn Sina, Ibn Yunus, al-Kashi, Ibn al-Haitham, 'Ali Ibn 'Isa al-Ghazali, al-zarqab, Omar Khayyam. A magnificent array of names which it would not be difficult to extend. If anyone tells you that the Middle Ages were scientifically sterile, just quote these men to him, all of whom flourished within a short period, 750 to 1100 A.D.[11]

A good example of these Islamic "Renaissance men" was the famous Ibn Sina Avicenna (d. 1037), who is known in the West as the Avicenna.

Ibn Sina (or Avicenna)

Ibn Sina was the son of a small administrator who lived near the city of Bukhara in Central Asia (now in the nation of Uzbekistan.) He is best known for his works in medicine and philosophy. His encyclopedic manual of medicine *al-Qanun fil-Tib* (*Canon in Medicine*) is often considered the most influential work in the history of medicine. Along with his philosophical encyclopedia *al-Shifa* (*The Book of Healing*), it was taught in major European universities until the sixteenth century.

By age ten, Avicenna had memorized the entire Qur'an and mastered the religious sciences of his time. At age thirteen, he began reading about medicine, and by the age of sixteen, he had mastered the field and began to practice as a physician.

Next, he started taking lessons on logic and metaphysics, and became a major expert in Greek, Persian, and Islamic philosophy. By age eighteen, he was a leading physician, philosopher, and astronomer. During the fifty-seven years of his life, he wrote numerous books, of which 240 have survived. Of these, one hundred fifty are on philosophy and forty are devoted to medicine, and the rest deal with subjects as varied as psychology, geology, mathematics, astronomy, and logic.

Muhamad ibn Musa al-Khwarizmi

Muhamad ibn Musa al-Khwarizmi (d. 846) was another name on George Sarton's list of great thinkers. He is known as the founder of algebra.

The term *algebra* is derived from the name of Muhamad ibn Musa al-Khwarizmi's famous book of algebra, *Kitab a-Jabr wal-Muqabalah* (literally meaning "the Book of Compulsion and Comparison"). The term *algorithm* comes from the European mispronunciation of his name. In *Kitab a-Jabr wal-Muqabalah*, written in the first quarter of the ninth century, Muhamad ibn Musa al-Khwarizmi for the first time brought all geometric and arithmetic problems into the form of algebraic operations, normal equations with standard solutions.

The mathematical theories of al-Khwarizmi were brought to their peak by another Renaissance man, the famous Persian poet, philosopher, and mathematician Umar (Omar) Khayyám. Though he is better known in the West for his ravishing book of poetry, *Rubaiyat*, he actually spent most of his life studying the sciences and he mastered many fields, particularly mathematics. He studied third-degree equations and elaborated on a workable universal geometric theory. His solutions, as well as his method of using auxiliary curves and geometric figures to solve third-degree operations, are often mistakenly attributed to French mathematician and philosopher René Descartes.

OMAR KHAYYÁM (c. 1048–1122)

Omar Khayyám was born at Nishapur, Iran. Early in his life, he developed interests in science and math—particularly algebra. Unlike many scientists of his time, he did not accept the patronage of a king; instead, he lived a quiet life searching for knowledge and traveling to great centers of learning, exchanging views with other scholars.

He made an attempt to classify most algebraic equations, including the third-degree equations and, in fact, offered solutions for a number of them. His book *Maqalat fi al-Jabr wa al-Muqabila* (*Articles on Algebra and Comparatives*) is a masterpiece that marked a major advancement in the development of algebra.

Omar Khayyám was the first to find the binomial theorem and to determine binomial coefficients. In geometry, he studied the generalities of the ancient Greek mathematician Euclid and contributed to the theory of parallel lines. At the request of a king, he produced a remarkably accurate solar calendar (*Al-Tarikh-al-Jalali*), which had an error of only one day in 3770 years, thus making it superior to the Gregorian calendar, which had an error of one day in 3330 years.

His other accomplishments include the development of methods for the accurate determination of specific gravity. In metaphysics, he wrote three books, and he also became a renowned astronomer and a physician. In the West, however, he is best known for his enchanting book of poetry, *Rubaiyat* (quatrains), translated into English by Edward Fitzgerald. Among his verses are these:

> *Some for the Glories of This World;*
> *and some Sigh for the Prophet's Paradise to come;*
> *Ah, take the Cash, and let the Credit go,*
> *Nor heed the rumble of a distant Drum! . . .*

> *I sometimes think that never blows so red*
> *The Rose as where some buried Caesar bled;*
> *That every Hyacinth the Garden wears Dropt*
> *in her Lap from some once lovely Head.* *

* Source: Available online at *http://www.poets.org/poems/poems.cfm?prmID=2490*.

Other Muslim Scientists

Muslim scientists were particularly interested in the field of astronomy and mathematical geography for practical reasons. The need for this knowledge stemmed from the requirements of worship rituals, such as prayers and fasting. Scientists had to determine the exact time prayers should be said; the times of sunrise, noon, and sunset for both prayers and fasting. They also had to find the direction of qiblah and the crescent moon visibility in order to determine the beginning and end of each lunar month.

Muslim scientists' calculation of the latitude and longitude of the earth for any given location was remarkably accurate; their results were comparable to results that would be reached today using modern advanced instruments.

8

Holidays

O ye who believe! Fasting is prescribed for you as it was
prescribed for those who preceded you, Maybe ye will
show piety. It is for a calculated number of days . . .
It is for the month of Ramadan. . . .

—The Qur'an 2:183

DIVERSITY OF HOLIDAYS

Holidays and festivals are important parts of any culture, and since Islam is a way of life for Muslim populations, many Muslim countries' holidays and festivals are religious in nature. Due to cultural differences between Muslim countries, however, the celebration of these religious holidays and festivals may not be uniform throughout the Muslim world. Muslim holidays celebrated in, say, Malaysia, will have a Malay flavor that distinguishes them from the same holidays celebrated in Iran, which will have a Persian flavor. Even among Arab Muslims, who share the same ethnicity and language, the national culture of each country has impacted the performance of religious rituals. The celebration of the same holiday may vary considerably from Morocco to Egypt to Saudi Arabia.

Besides cultural variations, different understandings of Islam have also had an influence on the celebration of major holidays. For example, whereas Egyptians, Turks, and Iranians lavishly celebrate the birthday of the prophet Muhammad, this event is often frowned upon by the more conservative Muslims of Saudi Arabia, the birthplace of the Prophet, who view the holiday as secular in origin. According to conservative Sunnis, putting too much emphasis on individuals prevents people from giving their full attention to God, and may even be perceived as a path toward idolatry. In addition to the Prophet's birthday, there are other festivals celebrated by Shiite Muslims that are not considered holidays by the Sunni majority. Examples are the birthdays and death days of the Prophet's family members and Shiite Muslim imams, and the day that Muhammad, according to Shiites, announced 'Ali as his successor, something Sunnis do not believe occurred. Since Islam follows a lunar calendar, Muslim holiday dates vary each year, as opposed to the Gregorian calendar used in the Western world.

ISLAMIC *HIJRI* CALENDAR

The Islamic calendar is based on lunar year. A lunar year generally follows the monthly cycles of the moon. A lunar month is determined by the period required for the moon to complete a full circle around the Earth, which takes about 29½ days. Twelve months of 29½ days each combine to make 354 days, the number of days in a lunar year. Based on these calculations, the Islamic lunar calendar is about eleven days shorter than the solar-based Gregorian calendar, which counts 365 days (366 in a leap year) because it is based on the movement of the Earth around the sun.

This eleven-day deficit causes each lunar month to move with the seasons, which are based on solar cycles. This means that important Muslim festivals, which always fall in the same month on the Islamic lunar calendar, may occur in different seasons based on the solar cycle. For instance, the fasting month of Ramadan could come in either winter or summer. Because of the eleven-day deficit of the lunar year, any given date on the Islamic calendar moves eleven days backward each year when measured on the solar-based Gregorian calendar. So, it takes about thirty-three years for a particular event on the Islamic calendar to complete its variations within seasons and occur again at approximately the same time on the solar calendar. For example, if the month of Ramadan occurred in October 2004 (on the Gregorian calendar), ten years later it will happen in July, and thirty-three years later it will be in October once again.

The Islamic Hijri calendar was introduced to the Muslim community in Medina in 638, during the caliphate of Umar ibn al-Khattab, the second caliph and a close companion of the prophet Muhammad. The dates of Islamic Hijri calendar in Western languages are usually abbreviated as "A.H." from the Latinized "*Anno Hegirae.*" This term meant "Year of the Hegira," with the word *Hegira* referring to Muhammad's flight from Mecca to Medina.

The Beginning of the Islamic Hijri Calendar

Interestingly, the Islamic calendar is not based on the birth of the Prophet, the major conquests of the Islamic Army, or even the day of the Prophet's first revelation. Instead, it starts on the day that the prophet Muhammad emigrated from Mecca to Medina, a major historical event and turning point in Islamic history that led to the formation of the first genuine Islamic community and city-state in Medina. The calendar, therefore, is based on the day that Muhammad decided to bring a new beginning to his mission by moving to a more sympathetic city, hoping to establish the community he envisioned based on God's guidance in the Qur'an and just principles.

As a result of its starting point, the calendar is called *Hijri*, a term derived from the word *hijrah*, meaning "emigration." The Islamic Hijri year starts at the first day of the month of Muharram (the first month of the year), which is roughly the equivalent of July 16, 622. The Muslim New Year 1425 started around February 22, 2004. Because the Islamic lunar calendar is eleven days shorter, it will eventually catch up to the Gregorian calendar. According to calculations done by specialists in the field, the fifth month of the year 20,874 on the Hijri calendar will also be the fifth month of the year 20,874 on the Gregorian calendar.[12]

Months of the Islamic Calendar

The Islamic months begin at the first sight of the new moon. Since the moon is seen at different times in different Muslim regions, there is no uniform beginning for months and years throughout the entire Islamic world. Most Muslims use the sighting of the new moon in their own location to determine the beginning of the new month. However, some Muslims consider the sighting of the new moon in Mecca, Saudi Arabia, the official beginning of each month, since Mecca is Islam's holiest city. The correct sighting is particularly important for performing religious rituals, such as the beginning and ending of fasting days during the month of Ramadan. The Qur'an refers to the significance of the phases of the moon for conducting religious rituals: "They ask you (Muhammad) of the new moons. Say: they are but signs to mark fixed periods of time in (the affairs of) mankind and for the pilgrimage . . ." (Q: 2:189). With regard to months of the year, the Qur'an states: "The number of months in the sight of God is twelve, so ordained by Him the day He created the heavens and the earth; of them four are sacred . . ." (Q. 9:36). For orthodox Muslims, a new month is considered to have begun only when it is announced by religious authorities who have seen the thin crescent moon with their own eyes. This makes marking the new month difficult when there is very low visibility.

The Islamic Hijri calendar contains twelve months that alternate between 29 and 30 days; the last month has 30 days only during leap years. A thirtieth day is added to the last month in eleven years out of every thirty-year cycle. Those years are the second, fifth, seventh, tenth, thirteenth, sixteenth, eighteenth, twenty-first, twenty-fourth, twenty-sixth, and twenty-ninth. The months of Islamic calendars are:

Month (Days)	
1	Muharram (30)
2	Safar (29)
3	Rabi'-ul awwal I (30)
4	Rabi'-ul thani II (29)
5	Jumada-ul awwal I (30)
6	Jumada-ul thani II (29)
7	Rajab (30)
8	Sha'ban (29)
9	Ramadan (30)
10	Shawwal (29)
11	Dhul Qa'da (30)
12	Dhul Hijjah (29; 30 days in leap years)

MUSLIM HOLIDAYS AND FESTIVALS

There are many holidays and festivals celebrated by Muslim communities throughout the world. Each one of these religious events has its own special spiritual significance for believers. The holidays are celebrated in various ways, depending on the cultural background of the Muslims who recognize them. The most common celebrations involve events such as street processions led by local religious and social leaders, the use of perfumes and burning scents, gathering in mosques or private houses to recite the Qur'an, and listening to religious music, stories, prose, and poetry about the particular event being celebrated.

Among all the holidays and festivals, there are two that are celebrated by all observing Muslims. They are referred to as *id* (*eid*), which simply means "festival," "feast," or literally, a "recurring happy occasion." These two major festivals are the *Id al-Adha*, or "Festival of Sacrifice," and *Id al-Fitr*, or "Festival of Breaking the Fast."

Id al-Adha (Festival of Sacrifice)

Id al-Adha is the most important Muslim festival. It is referred to as the *Id al-Kabir*, or "Great Festival." It starts on the tenth day of Dhul Hijjah, the last month of the Islamic calendar, and lasts four days. It marks the official end of the hajj (pilgrimage to Mecca). Those who are lucky enough to be in Mecca at the proper time celebrate the festival with their fellow pilgrims; those who could not make the trip join their local Muslim community members to celebrate the event.

Id al-Adha is called the Festival of Sacrifice because those who can afford to do so are supposed to sacrifice an animal. The animal can be chosen from any that is allowed by Islamic law; it should be a healthy, full-grown animal. If a sheep or goat is used, one animal should be sacrificed on behalf of a household; a larger animal such as a cow or camel, however, may fulfill the sacrificial obligations of up to seven households.

The sacrifice ceremony involves communal prayers at a mosque or a *musallah* (a prayer house usually located outside of

Holiday	Islamic Month in Which Holiday Falls	2004	2005	2006	2007
Id al-Adha	Dhul Hijjah	Sunday February 1	Friday January 21	Sunday December 31	Thursday December 20
Islamic New Year	Muharram	Sunday February 22	Thursday February 10	Tuesday January 31	Saturday January 20
Prophet's Birthday	Rabi' ul awwal	Sunday May 2	Thursday April 21	Tuesday April 11	Saturday March 31
Isra & Miraj	Rajab	Saturday September 11	Thursday September 1	Monday August 21	Friday August 10
Ramadan	Ramadan	Saturday October 16	Wednesday October 5	Sunday September 24	Thursday September 13
Id al-Fitr	Shawwal	Sunday November 14	Friday November 4	Tuesday October 24	Saturday October 14

the city), or at any other place designed for the occasion. Believers say prayers containing at least two ra'kats.

After prayers, there is a sermon by the imam, in which he explains the roots of the festival. He narrates the story of how Abraham was commanded by God to sacrifice his beloved son Ishmael. As Abraham was about to carry out God's orders, God showed mercy and sent the archangel Gabriel to stop Abraham, bringing a white lamb to be sacrificed instead. So, like Abraham, who sacrificed the lamb in place of his son, devout Muslims who have the financial means should sacrifice an animal to demonstrate their appreciation of God's mercy and generosity.

After the sermon is over, participants begin to chant and sing, praising God. They chant: "God is Great, God is Great; There is no deity but God; God is Great, God is Great; all praise belongs to God." Then they return home to sacrifice their prepared animals.

Families usually sacrifice the animal in front of their own houses. They water the animal, then, while praising God, they use a sharp knife to kill the animal. The meat is then divided into three equal shares. The person who physically offered the sacrifice is allowed to take one-third. The other two shares go to relatives, friends, and the poor. Millions of animals are slaughtered throughout the Muslim world during this four-day festival. This is the time that the wealthy share some of their good fortune with the poor.

During the hajj season, more than 2 million faithful Muslims gather in Mecca each year and, as part of the required hajj rituals, they are supposed to offer the traditional sacrifice. Having so many animals sacrificed becomes a very difficult task, however, so to make the festival's requirements more workable, many pilgrims give the monetary equivalent of the sacrificial animals to charitable organizations that will reach the poor, which is the main intention of the sacrifice.

Some Sufis contend that the sacrificial animal represents the animal nature within human beings that should be sacrificed so that the faithful can reach the state of purity, required in their path toward God. The Qur'an speaks of the motives behind the sacrifice: "Neither the flesh nor the blood of your sacrifices reaches God, but it is the righteous motive underlying them that reaches Him. He has made them subject to you that you may glorify God for His guidance to you. So give the good news to those who are doers of good" (Q. 22:37).

Id al-Fitr (Festival of Breaking the Fast)

Id al-Fitr is celebrated at the end of the Ramadan. The festival marks the end of a full month of fasting. The festival starts when the new moon has been officially sighted, and the celebration continues for three days. It is a joyous occasion to pay tribute to God's bounty and benevolence. It is an occasion to celebrate life, eat good food, wear nice clothing, decorate the home, prepare special foods and sweets, and entertain guests. Children in particular are dressed well, and they traditionally receive money and gifts from their parents and relatives. Id al-Fitr is also a period for visiting relatives and friends, and especially those who are sick or in need. It is a time to exchange gifts and feed the poor.

Although Id al-Fitr is a merry occasion, it is not a time for believers to indulge in fickleness or overindulgence. Instead, Id al-Fitr is a time to reflect on one's spiritual needs and relations with God. And more importantly, it is a time to remember one's duties to the community and obligations toward the poor.

Custom requires that each head of household should carefully calculate the family's income and revenue for the previous year and allocate part as *Sadaqat-ul-Fitr* or *Fitrana* ("Id-al-Fitr charity") for the benefit of the poor. This contribution is made on behalf of the family as a way of showing gratitude to God for his support during the last year. Usually, the donation will reach the poor before Id al-Fitr begins, which allows them to participate in this happy event without being empty-handed. [13]

Laylat al-Qadr ("Night of the Power")

The Qur'an equates this night with a thousand months: "We have indeed revealed this (Qur'an) in the Night of Power. And what will explain what the Night of Power is? The Night of Power is better than a thousand months. Therein come down the angels and the Spirit (Gabriel) by God's permission, on every errand: Peace! until the appearance of dawn" (Q. 97:1–5).

The Night of Power is celebrated on the twenty-seventh night of Ramadan. However, according to the Prophet himself, any of the odd-numbered nights of the last ten days of Ramadan may have been the Night of Power.

Ramadan

Ramadan is sacred for Muslims throughout the world. It is the month of fasting, the month for purification of the soul, for remembrance of God through sincere prayers, and a time for repentance. During Ramadan, Muslims recite the Qur'an regularly, and it is recommended that the entire Qur'an be read at least once during the month.

Many devout Muslims who can afford to take the time away from work and other obligations retreat to a mosque for the last ten days and nights of Ramadan and devote all of their attention to God, just as Muhammad himself was known to do. During these times of retreat (*i'tikaf*), Muslims fast during the day and occupy themselves with venerating God through voluntary prayers and reflection on the words of the Qur'an, both day and night. Many people do not leave the mosque except in cases of urgent need. The faithful are supplied with food and other possible needs by family members or the custodians of the mosque.

Ramadan is also a month of sharing one's resources with the poor, as in the festival of Id al-Fitr. For many Muslims, it is also a time to celebrate life and its amenities as God-given gifts.

Not everybody retreats to a mosque on the nights of Ramadan. For many people, the nights of Ramadan, after fasting the whole day, are an occasion to enjoy life, visit relatives and friends, eat in restaurants, see plays with religious themes, listen to music, and watch television. In Egypt, it is customary for television stations to reserve some of their best programming for the nights of Ramadan when people usually stay up later and watch television with friends and relatives.

Milad al-Nabi (The Birthday of the Prophet)

Milad al-Nabi, or *Mawlid al-Nabi*, is the commemoration of the prophet Muhammad's birthday, which takes place on the twelfth day of Rabi' ul-awwal, the third month of the Islamic calendar. In the eyes of many Muslims around the world, Muhammad is the ideal man, the perfect human being who should be emulated for his God-like qualities. Muhammad was both a religious and political leader. He was also a revolutionary for his time—the man who stood against age-old inhumane pagan practices and preached justice and equality for all people regardless of race, ethnicity, gender, or family connections. Most important of all, he was the one chosen by God to be the last great prophet on Earth. Through him, the message of Islam was announced to all of humanity.

Many Muslims celebrate this holiday by decorating the streets and public places and organizing speeches and lectures about the life and sayings of the Prophet. They also recite the Qur'an and read prose and poetry praising the Prophet. Following recitation of the Qur'an and poetry readings, sweets are distributed, and perfume is offered or sprinkled on worshipers. Music is played all over the city.

Since the death of the Prophet is also believed to have taken place on the same date, Muslims are careful not to go too far with their music and joy on the occasion of Milad al-Nabi. They strive to keep a balance in their celebrations and always remember the Prophet's wise saying, "Live in this life like if you live for ever; live in this life like if you die tomorrow; the balance to this is Islam." Muhammad had offered his followers a religion of balance between *deen* (religious life) and *donya* (secular life). He advised them to enjoy life on Earth but never to forget about the life to come (and for which they must prepare) after death.

Though all Muslims are thankful for the birth of the prophet Muhammad, not all Muslims celebrate his birthday. Some conservative Muslims, such as the Wahhabis of Saudi Arabia, consider the celebration of birthdays a modern innovation, which has no precedent in the early history of Islam and therefore is not condoned by the Qur'an or hadith. To make their case, they refer to the Prophet's advising the faithful to avoid innovations for fear of misguidance. Despite their attitude, there have been many scholars who did not think all innovations were unworthy or harmful. They considered the good innovations—those that do not contradict the Qur'an—praiseworthy. So, in their view, the celebration of Muhammad's birthday uplifts believers and pleases God. The Qur'an states: "God and his angels send blessings on the Prophet. You who believe send your blessing on him as well, and salute him with respect" (Q. 33:56).

Lailat al-Isra wa al-Mi'raj
(The Night of the Journey and the Ascension)

Muslims commemorate the night that, according to Islamic tradition, the prophet Muhammad, through a journey guided by the archangel Gabriel, ascended to heaven to meet with God. The tradition continues that, on the way to see God, the Prophet met Adam, Abraham, Moses, Jesus, and some other prophets. When he was about to approach God, Gabriel faced the Prophet and remarked that, as an angel, he was not allowed to go any further, but Muhammad could continue his ascendance. Muhammad reached God and drank from the fountain of spiritual knowledge. Upon his return to Earth, he brought with him the divinely inspired wisdom that made him such a great teacher and inspiration. It was during this journey that he was given God's instructions for the five daily prayers.

The event of Mi'raj, according to Muslim scholars, was a spiritual journey, a journey that signifies the origin of the Prophet's incredible insight and wisdom. The ascent took place in Mecca on the twenty-seventh day of Rajab, the seventh month of Islamic calendar, two years before Muhammad's emigration to Medina.

Mi'raj is a joyful occasion. Houses, streets, and religious buildings are decorated with colorful flags and signs and, at night, bright lights illuminate them. Toward evening, believers assemble in mosques to listen to speeches about the life of the Prophet and to participate in group prayers, chanting and singing in praise of Muhammad. After the speeches, religious songs, and prayers are over, sweets are distributed and perfume is sprinkled on participants. Money is also collected to be distributed among the poor.

Other Festivals

There are several other festivals and observances that are celebrated by Muslims. Some of them are actually pre-Islamic holidays, but they have gained an Islamic flavor as a result of contact with the ever-growing Muslim population. For example, the *Norooz*, or Iranian New Year, which happens at the spring equinox, is a major festival celebrated for thirteen days in Iran, Afghanistan, Tajikistan, Turkey, and other areas that are under the influence of Iranian culture. Although this is a national, not a religious, holiday, even during the Norooz celebration at the moment the year is changing, many devout Iranians recite the holy Qur'an and remember God as their sustainer.

Events commemorated by the Shiite Muslim population include *Ashrah*, the tenth day in the month of Muharram, which recalls the day in 680 when Husayn (Hussein), the grandson of the Prophet, and members of his family were massacred on the orders of Yazid, the second Umayyad caliph. A happier occasion is the day that Muhammad, according to Shiite tradition, proclaimed 'Ali, his cousin and son-in-law, as his successor. This event is known as *Id al-Ghadir*, which, according to Shiites, happened on the eighteenth of Dhul Hijjah, three months before the death of the Prophet in 632.

9

Memories

*Being upright does not consist in turning your
faces to the East or to the West, but being upright
is to believe in Allah, and the Last Day, and the
angels, and the Books, and the Prophets. . . .*

—The Qur'an 2:177

THE SPREAD OF ISLAM

Within a century of the prophet Muhammad's death, Islam had become a world empire that stretched from North Africa to Southeast Asia. Mosques, Islam's main religious and cultural landmarks, could be seen all over the world from Asia to Africa to Europe. The Islamic Empire reached a scope that rivaled that of the Roman Empire at its peak. It spanned 3,000 miles from east to west, covering areas from the Pyrenees on the border of France to the Pamirs in Central Asia, from North Africa and Egypt to the Byzantine territory south of the Taurus Mountains, and the Persian Empire in the East.

For many people, especially those from Western cultures, it was hard to understand (and still is) how an ideology that emerged among a small group of Arab tribes, within less than a century, could become a world ideology adopted by people from sophisticated cultures. Faithful Muslims, however, interpreted this rapid expansion of Islam as divine intervention. The idea that God was behind them inspired many Muslim caliphs and rulers to take additional risks and spread the word of God (which they viewed as their mission) to faraway places. They called their military conquest *fath*, an Arabic term meaning "opening" or "victory" for the transfer of Islam. They sincerely believed that humanity would benefit from being exposed to the ideals of Islam. At the same time, they believed they would reserve a place for themselves in paradise by spreading God's word as it was revealed to the Prophet.

To these early military rulers, spreading the worldview of Islam was a good deed, especially when they were dealing with territories that either lacked a sound spiritual ideology or had a religious tradition that was very corrupt. For example, political corruption and moral bankruptcy within the two major empires of the time, the Sassanid (Persian Zoroastrian Empire) the Byzantine (the Christian Eastern Roman Empire), made them too weak to resist the advancing Islamic armies. In addition, hundreds of years of power struggles and bloody battles between the two empires of Sassanids and Byzantines left the people on both sides exhausted and eager for change. Dissatisfaction with their political rulers, extreme poverty, and the stratified societies sanctioned by the law did not give the people of these empires enough incentive to defend their territories against the Muslim invaders. For many, it was simply a matter of exchanging one master for another, with the hope that the new master would be more benevolent. Many people, of course, had heard about the new Islamic religion of Arabia that called for the oneness of humanity and equality of all races in the sight of God; those who had heard the news generally welcomed the idea of being ruled by Muslims. Many, in fact, quickly accepted the new religion.

It is interesting to note that neither of the religions practiced by these empires—the Christianity of the Byzantines or the Zoroastrianism of Persia—was inherently corrupt. However, the way these two religions had been exploited by a group of opportunistic leaders over time made them appear corrupt to the populace. Power-hungry religious leaders had alienated themselves from the public by aligning themselves with the overtly corrupt kings and emperors and sanctioning their cruel rule over their subjects. This behavior stood in sharp contrast with that of the early Islamic leaders, who considered themselves the servants of God and protectors of the faithful.

The fall of the Sassanid and Byzantine empires brought vast new territories under Muslim rule. Soon, Iraq, Syria, Palestine, Persia, and Egypt had become Islamic territories. The Western borders of the empire reached Spain and Morocco and expanded across Central Asia all the way to India.

The defeated population was given two choices: to accept Islam as their religion and enjoy the full membership of Islamic community, or to continue to observe their own religion and pay a poll tax (*jizyah*) to the conquerors. By paying jizyah, the new subjects became part of the protected people (*dhimmi*). The dhimmi were exempt from military service and were protected against potential outside aggressors. They also were not responsible for paying *zakat*, the religious tax that Muslims were required to pay. Although some of the conquered population converted to Islam solely to escape paying the jizyah, it is not correct to assume that economic reasons were the only motives behind the rapid conversions of conquered peoples to Islam. Many were very sincere in their acceptance of Islam; in fact, quite a few converts later became major scholars of Islamic law and theology.

Christian and Jews were considered "People of the Book" and were respected as monotheistic fellows who had their own sacred revelations. They were therefore given full protection and liberty to practice their religious rituals in their churches and synagogues. Many sects—including Nestorians, Jacobites, and Copts—that had been labeled heretic by the Christian Orthodoxy under the rule of Byzantium welcomed the Muslim rulers as their saviors. Because Muslims saw Islam as a continuation of the Judeo-Christian tradition, they had great respect for Jewish and Christian cultures. However, this did not mean that Jews and Christians were never mistreated under Muslim rulers. Some closed-minded rulers who had little understanding of other religions made life very difficult for their non-Muslim subjects. Generally speaking, though, the majority of Muslim rulers acted according to the Qur'anic passage, "there is no compulsion in religion," and treated their non-Muslim subjects fairly, allowing them to establish flourishing communities within the Islamic Empire. Some members of these religious minorities became important scientists, philosophers, and political administrators under the patronage of Muslim rulers.

Although military conquests helped the growth of Islam, it was not by any means the only reason for Islamic expansion. In fact, regions that today contain the largest Muslim countries, such as Southeast Asia (where the largest Islamic country, Indonesia, is located), never faced an Islamic army. The spread of Islam to these regions and to most of Africa, which today contains a significant number of Muslims, occurred through trade and the efforts of Sufi masters. As early as the twelfth and thirteenth centuries, Islamic merchants and mystics introduced people throughout the Malay-Indonesian archipelago to Islam, mainly through peaceful means. Today, there is a sizable Muslim population in Malaysia, Brunei, Indonesia, and the southern parts of Philippines and Thailand.

THE DEVELOPMENT OF ISLAMIC SOCIETY

From the time of the Prophet, religion and politics were intertwined. In addition to being recognized as the Messenger of God, Muhammad was known for his political shrewdness, administrative wisdom, and military strategy. He was a diplomat who set an example as a good statesman for his successors to follow. His community-state in Medina, which he based on faith

WHAT IS JIHAD?

In the West, the term *jihad* usually carries with it a negative connotation. It is used to describe the violent side of Islam. However, contrary to this popular Western opinion, *jihad* actually means to strive to be a good Muslim and to follow the path of God.

According to Islam, temptation to do evil is the strongest of a person's enemies, so the "greater jihad" is the struggle to overcome immoral temptations and conquer one's ego. Jihad also means to do good and prevent evil, and to spread the word of God, mainly through peaceful means. It is the "lesser jihad" by which God commands Muslims to defend their faith, home, and community, even if they have to use arms. Even then, however, God does not like the aggressors: "And fight with them until there is no oppression, and there prevail justice and faith in God; but if they cease, let there be no hostility except to those who practise oppression" (Q. 2:193).

When the Prophet and his army returned victorious from the Battle of Badr in A.D. 624, Muhammad faced his followers and declared: "today you have won the 'lesser jihad,' but now you have your main task ahead of you, the 'greater jihad', following the straight path."

Some Muslim political activists, in order to justify their terrorist acts and gain sympathy from their fellow Muslims, have recently exploited the concept of jihad. Those who understand the true meaning of jihad know it cannot be expanded to justify the murder of innocent people in an offensive act, as happened in the terrorist attacks of September 11, 2001.

and governmental order, was a success. Politics, law, education, social service, and the whole fabric of society were based on teachings of the Qur'an and consideration of the common good. Under Muhammad's guidance, the community learned how to function as a unit. Circumstances such as early feuds with opponents in Mecca taught the people that if they wanted to survive as a community, they would have to function as a united body. This idea of making the community the first priority helped the Muslims to prosper as a successful city-state and, later, as a world empire.

THE PRISTINE ISLAM: THE FOUR RIGHTLY GUIDED CALIPHS

The idea of Muhammad's being the seal of the prophets brought an end to the tradition of prophethood after his death in 632. Since Muhammad's political authority was believed to have been bestowed upon him by God, whoever became the next leader would inherit his divine mandate, but would not enjoy the same authority. Since, according to popular view, Muhammad did not clearly delineate a successor before he died, his death brought confusion about who should follow in the footsteps of such a great leader. This confusion gradually led to a crisis, which split the community into Shiite and Sunni divisions—a separation that exists to the present day. In accordance with Arab custom of the time, after the death of the Prophet, a group of tribal elders gathered and selected Abu Bakr, Muhammad's close friend and father-in-law to be the next Muslim leader. The leader was to be called *caliph* (*khalifah*), meaning the "deputy," or, in this case, "deputy of the Prophet."

Abu Bakr, known as the first adult male who converted to Islam, was a respectable man and was liked by many. However, a group of Muslims expressed dissatisfaction with his selection and believed that 'Ali, Muhammad's cousin and son-in-law, should be the first caliph after Muhammad. They claimed that Muhammad, in his last pilgrimage on the way from Medina to Mecca, stopped by a place called Ghadir Khumm and introduced

'Ali to the community there as his successor. This claim was not accepted by a majority, however, and Abu Bakr became the first official caliph.

Abu Bakr was an old man, so his reign, which began in 632, was brief; he died after two and a half years in office. During his reign, Abu Bakr managed to put down insurgencies by local tribes, consolidated the tribes of Arabia, and established the rule of Islam over the entire Arabian Peninsula. Before his death, Abu Bakr, to avoid the same confusion that had occurred when Muhammad died, named 'Umar ibn al-Khattab as his successor.

During the reign of 'Umar (634–644), the Muslim Army defeated the Persian Sassanid and Eastern Roman Byzantine empires, and Islam spread to Persia, Iraq, Syria, and North Africa. 'Umar was generous with conquered people and showed great respect for Christians and Jews and their places of worship when his army captured the city of Jerusalem. He also institutionalized the Hijri Islamic calendar throughout territories ruled by the Islamic Empire. 'Umar was known for his personal integrity, frugality, and sense of justice. He called himself "the Commander of Faithful" (*Amir ul Mu'minin*). In 644, his life came to an abrupt end when his servant, who had a personal grudge against 'Umar, stabbed him to death.

Following 'Umar, the two main candidates for caliph were 'Uthman ibn Affan and 'Ali ibn Abi Talib; the elders chose 'Uthman to be the next leader. Unlike his predecessors, 'Uthman belonged to the influential Umayyad clan that had once challenged the prophet Muhammad in Mecca. Though 'Uthman was a pious man, he was prone to nepotism. When he appointed a close relative as the governor of Egypt, he caused a controversy. People who were unhappy with the governor of Egypt complained about him and asked for his resignation. When 'Uthman ignored their demands, an angry mob surrounded his house and killed him. The greatest accomplishment of 'Uthman's reign (644–656) was his appointment of a group of experts to collect all existing copies of the Qur'an and establish the standard text for future Muslim generations.

After 'Uthman's death, 'Ali was finally selected by the elders to be the fourth and last caliph. As might have been expected, 'Ali's reign (656–661) was turbulent. The community was already divided into Shiite and Sunni communities, with southern Iraq and Iran being heavily influenced by Shiism. After overcoming some rebellious movements against his rule, 'Ali moved his capital to Kufah, a garrison city in southern Iraq where he had many supporters. 'Ali was a devoutly religious man but he was not a politician. He was too rigid and idealistic in his beliefs to compromise when he thought he was right. He was not equipped to be a good diplomat, which is sometimes key to political survival.

The death of 'Uthman still remained a problem. 'Uthman's nephew Mu'awiya, who had been appointed governor of Syria, wanted 'Ali to punish the assassins of his uncle. When 'Ali refused, Mu'awiya started a war against him. The two armies met at Saffin on the upper Euphrates River, on the frontier between Iraq and Syria. Just as the battle was turning in 'Ali's favor, Mu'awiya's soldiers raised the pages of the Qur'an on their spears and called for God to judge among people through a mutually agreed arbitration. Against the advice of some of his associates and staunch supporters, 'Ali agreed to the arbitration, in which he lost his claim to the caliphate. The arbitration ruled against him and wanted Mu'awiya to be the legitimate caliph. Although 'Ali refused to accept the result, the armies retreated. The conflict between the two sides continued until a member of an opposing group assassinated 'Ali when he was leading prayers in the mosque of Kufah.

THE *KHARIJIS* (*KHAWARIJ*) OR "DISSENTERS"
Khawarij (single form is *Khariji*), known as *Kharijis* (*Kharijites*) in the West, were the first radical, or "fundamentalist," [14] group within Islam. Understanding this group will help us to better understand the contemporary radical groups such as Takfir wa Hijiah, Jihad al-Islami, and al-Qaeda.

When Mu'awiya's army lifted copies of the Qur'an during the Battle of Saffin and asked for arbitration to decide whether

'Ali or Mu'awiya should be caliph, some of 'Ali's followers considered this action deceitful. They declared that God would select the legitimate ruler by helping the righteous group win the battle. In this faction's view, 'Ali was the inheritor of Muhammad's divine mandate and should not compromise with those who challenged his rule. When 'Ali accepted the arbitration against their wishes, they took it as an act of unbelief (*kufr*) and turned against 'Ali, declaring his caliphate illegitimate. Their slogan was, "No judgment but God's judgment." They chose to withdraw from the rest of the Muslim world as Muhammad had withdrawn from the godless Meccan community. They became known as *Khawarij*, meaning "seceders" or "dissenters." They banded together as an armed group and began a program of sabotage and assassination against those they regarded as unbelievers.

Khawarij, like some of today's radical fundamentalists, were extremists. They were very pious and they killed in the name of God. They called themselves *shurat*, or "those who give their lives for God." They believed that killing in God's name would reserve a place for them in paradise (Q. 9:111). They criticized the popular belief of the time that the caliph should come from the Quraysh tribe; they claimed this was a deviation from teachings of the Qur'an. In their opinion, anyone could become a caliph—even a black African slave. They believed that Muslims who committed major sins were unbelievers and that their blood should be shed and their properties, wives, and children taken as war booty (the former Taliban in Afghanistan sometimes used this same practice).

Khawarij saw the world in terms of black and white; the world was strictly divided between believers and unbelievers, Muslims and non-Muslims, peace and warfare. They had no patience for compromise. Their interpretation of the Qur'an was very literal and showed no understanding of the dynamics and circumstances under which some of the verses were originally revealed. Basing their actions on this erroneous view of Islam, they killed indiscriminately and justified their deeds in the name of God.

They had no concept of a merciful God who loves compassion and declared that "there is no compulsion in religion."

'Ali made repeated attempts to bring back the Khawarij back to the regular community of Muslims, but he was unsuccessful. So, he had to fight them in the Battle of Nahrawan (658). The Khawarij were defeated in this battle, but that only made their urge and desire for martyrdom stronger. Three years later, one of the Khawarij murdered 'Ali with a poisoned sword as he was about to lead morning prayers. There were Khawarij plots to kill both Mu'awiya and Amr ibn As on the same day, but the men in charge of them were arrested and executed before they could carry out their plans. Despite this setback, the Khawarij continued their guerrilla warfare against the Umayyad and Abbasid caliphs.

THE UMAYYAD EMPIRE (661–750)

With 'Ali out of the picture, Mu'awiya proclaimed himself the next caliph. There was some opposition to his announcement from Hasan, 'Ali's older son, who also claimed the caliphate. After he realized that Mu'awiya's followers were more powerful than his own, Hasan signed a peace agreement and prevented unnecessary bloodshed. Mu'awiya moved the capital to Damascus, where he had been stationed when he was governor of Syria.

A competent politician, he managed to neutralize his opposition and established a peace that lasted for most of his reign (661–680). The shift of the Islamic seat of political power to Damascus, a major Greco-Roman city, changed the aim and reality of the caliphate. Mu'awiya, the son of Abu Sufiyan, who had once been an archenemy of the Prophet, was now in charge of the Islamic state that would soon become an empire. He managed to change the system of caliphate to a sultanate, meaning that leadership became hereditary, based on blood connections—a tradition that the prophet Muhammad had struggled to prevent.

Mu'awiya turned the caliphate into a dynasty, a monopoly of Bani Umayyad (his children), and excluded non-Arabs from high offices, to the extent that the state became known as the Arab Kingdom. This was all against the concept of egalitarianism advocated by Islam. So, by 680, when Yazid replaced his father, Mu'awiya, as sultan, there was a large degree of dissatisfaction against Umayyad rule, and especially against Yazid himself, who was known as a drunk by the Shiites of southern Iraq.

A group of disgruntled Muslims from Kufah in southern Iraq invited Husayn (Hussein), the younger son of 'Ali and the grandson of Prophet, to lead them in a resistance movement against Yazid. After some hesitation, Husayn accepted the invitation and left Medina for Kufah to join his supporters. On his way to Kufah, he and more than seventy of his family members and supporters were stopped on the plain of Karbala on the bank of the Euphrates River by an army dispatched by the Yazid's governor in Kufah. Yazid's representative offered Husayn powerful governmental positions in exchange for his loyalty. Husayn was an idealist, however; he did not accept. Even though he knew his people could not win the battle, he still chose to fight Yazid's army. He chose death over compromise with what he considered the immoral and corrupt government of Yazid.

On the tenth day of the Muharram of 680, a day known as Ashura, Husayn and the male members of his family were massacred. The women and one of his sons (Zain al-Abidin), who was sick at the time, were taken as captives. This event in Shiite history is remembered as the "Tragedy of Karbala," or "Husayn's Ashura." For Shiites, Husayn's battle against Yazid symbolizes the struggle of good versus evil, innocent versus tyrant. Since the event, Shiite Muslims have commemorated the massacre every year during the month of Muharram, which they consider the month of mourning.

Despite problems that arose during the early caliphates, the Umayyads are known for their military, political, administrative, and cultural achievements. The Islamic Empire flourished and became stable under reign of later caliphs, such as Abd al-Malik ibn Marvan and Umar ibn Abd al-Aziz. The Umayyads managed to build the first Islamic fleet and to become a maritime power.

They dominated the Mediterranean and sailed east to India and west to Spain. They secured the waterways throughout their territories so that seafarers and other merchants could move safely and easily within the empire. Thanks to this freedom in transportation, seafarers carried Islam all the way to India and China.

Among the Umayyads' cultural achievements were the building of monuments such as the Dome of the Rock in Jerusalem and the great Umayyad Mosque of Damascus. The Arabic writing of the Qur'an was standardized for educational purposes. The administration systems inherited from the conquered subjects were changed to fit the Islamic method of government, while Arab coins became the standard monetary unit of the entire empire.

The Umayyads gradually began to lose support, especially among the non-Arab population. Due to their dynastic nature and emphasis on "Arabness," many considered them Arab rather than Islamic rulers. Those non-Arabs who had accepted Islam as their religion had to attach themselves to an Arab tribe in order to be recognized and protected, but they were still treated as second-class citizens and were subject to higher taxes than the Arab Muslims. Many people found these rules unjust and believed that they went against the ideals of Islam, so they began to resist the later Umayyad caliphs. Opposition was particularly fierce in the regions most remote from Damascus and in areas populated by non-Arabs and Shiites. In the province of Khorasan in eastern Iran, a major resistance movement grew under the leadership of a charismatic Persian general known as Abu Muslim. Abu Muslim and his followers, who were called *Seyah Jamegan*

THE DOME OF THE ROCK

One of the best-known holy Muslim structures is the Dome of the Rock in Jerusalem. The oldest surviving Muslim building that is still intact in its original form, it holds a large rock from which Muhammad is said to have ascended to heaven at the end of his legendary night journey.

(meaning "men in black cloth"), were Shiites who wanted to shift political power back to the family of Muhammad. They supported one of the descendants of Abbas, Muhammad's uncle, giving them the name "Abbasids." In 750, with the help of Abu Muslim, the opposition drove the Umayyads from power and the Abbasids took over.

THE ABBASIDS (750–1258)

Since the Abbasids rose to power with the help of sympathizers in Iraq and Iran (Persia), it was natural for them to move their capital to where they had the most support. Al-Mansur, the second Abbasid caliph built the city of Baghdad (located in present-day Iraq) in 762 on the Tigris River near Ctesiphon, the ancient capital of the Sassanid (Persian) Empire. He called the city *Madinat a-Salam*, meaning "the City of Peace." A round-shaped fortified city, Baghdad was built at a central point between Syria in the west, Arabia in the south, and Persia in the east. During the next caliphate, Baghdad grew significantly, and by the ninth and tenth centuries, it had become the jewel of the Islamic Empire. At that time, it was the greatest commercial, educational, and cultural center in the world.

By the time the Abbasids came to power, the Islamic community was ethnically and linguistically diverse. The Abbasids used this diversity to their advantage and built an empire based on the experience of many varied cultures. They employed bright individuals from different ethnic back-grounds. They utilized the services of experienced Persian and Greek bureaucrats and intellectuals and reformed their court and administration systems. Abbasid caliphs—especially Harun al-Rashid and his son Ma'mun—became patrons of art, literature, and science, and gave generous grants to qualified scholars. With the help of their Persian chief ministers, they emulated the administrative systems that had brought success in earlier times to Persian rulers. Caliph al-Ma'mun (who reigned 813–833) built the official educational institution in Baghdad, the *Bayt al-Hikma* (House of Wisdom). It became a haven for scholars from all over the world who wanted a suitable place to pursue their studies.

The class of religious scholars known as 'ulama also emerged during the Abbasid period. Since Islam does not recognize any official clergy or priesthood, 'ulama are the people most qualified to interpret Islamic texts. As a professional elite who could interpret the Qur'an, ahadith, and the shari'ah, 'ulama became an influential and respected social class. Abbasids (who called themselves the preservers of Prophet's tradition) supported the development of Islamic scholarship and became patrons of scholars who worked on developing the shari'ah. Under their patronage, the early law schools that began to develop during the late Umayyad period flourished and, with the help of 'ulama, they codified major laws, making rules applicable everywhere throughout the Islamic Empire.

Gradually, the Abbasid caliphate started to show signs of disintegration. Turkish groups who were originally brought from Central Asia to guard the caliphs against Persian and Arab rivals became too powerful and began to dominate the caliphate. The empire was growing too large and had too many ambitious generals who had an eye on gaining power for themselves in Baghdad. As the Abbasids became weaker, some of the caliphs became pawns in the hands of their generals. Ethnic rivalry and disobedience of the orders of caliphs became the norm. The Abbasids were no longer able to hold their subjects together, and territories began to break away from the empire. Non-Arab Muslims began to demand a voice in the administration of state and society. Non-Arab Muslims in the West, Spain, North Africa, and eventually Egypt, rebelled against imperial control and went their own way. In the East, Persia grew strong enough to become master of its own lands. The empire became fragmented, and by 945, a Shiite Persian dynasty, the Buyids, captured Baghdad and forced the Abbasid caliph to endorse their rule. The Buyids ruled for over a century (945–1055), during which time they patronized the study of Shiism and helped develop Shiite hadith tradition, theology, and jurisprudence.

With the fragmentation of the empire, new centers of power began to emerge. Other cultural centers in Persia, Central Asia, Spain, and North Africa emerged as rivals to Baghdad. In each of these places, scholars were supported by the rulers of various dynasties. The Arabic language lost its grip as the official language of scholarship; other tongues began to flourish under the patronage of nationalistic rulers. A large body of Islamic literature, for instance, was written in Persian.

Though they had lost control over the empire, the Abbasid caliphs, as descendants of the Prophet, remained as nominal leadership figures. They were used as a source of legitimacy for the various regional rulers who controlled different parts of the former empire.

THE MONGOLS AND THEIR AFTERMATH

The eastern lands of Islam, including Persia, Iraq, Syria, and Palestine, were devastated by Changiz (Genghis) Khan and his descendants. They poured out of Central Asia and sacked cities wherever they passed. In 1258, the grandson of Changiz Khan, Hulagu Khan, reached Baghdad. Historian Sir John Bagot Glubb explained, "For five hundred years, Baghdad had been a city of palaces, mosques, libraries and colleges. Its universities and hospitals were the most up-to-date in the world. Nothing now remained but heaps of rubble and a stench of decaying human flesh." [15] After destroying the city completely, Hulagu Khan massacred its Muslim population and murdered the last Abbasid caliph and his family.

The Mongols continued their pillage, going west until the Mamluks of Egypt in the Sinai Peninsula finally stopped them. Although the Mongol invasion was at first devastating to Islam and the Muslims, gradually, the Mongols' later descendants accepted Islam as their religion and became generous patrons of Islamic art, science, and shari'ah.

By the middle of sixteenth century, once again there were three major Muslim empires emerging in the Islamic world. Their combined domain of influence stretched from North

Africa to the eastern borders of the Indian subcontinent. The Turkish Ottoman Empire (1517–1923), stationed in Istanbul, controlled a vast area including the Anatolian Peninsula, a good portion of the Arab Middle East and North Africa, and the Balkan Peninsula. The Persian Safavid Empire (1501–1723) was stationed in Esfahān (Isfahan), Iran, and controlled what are today Iran, southern Iraq, Afghanistan, and parts of Central Asia. Finally, the Indian Mughal Empire (1483–1857), which was centered in Delhi, India, controlled most of the Indian subcontinent, including what is today India, Pakistan, and Bangladesh. Under these great empires, peace and tranquillity once again returned to Islamic lands, and art, science, and literature thrived.

10

Islam in the World Today

*The doctrine of brotherhood of Islam extends to all
human beings, no matter what color, race or creed. Islam
is the only religion which has been able to realize this
doctrine in practice. Muslims wherever on the world
they are will recognize each other as brothers*

—R.L. Mellema, Dutch anthropologist,
writer, and scholar

ISLAM AND THE CHRISTIAN WEST

Although Islam and Christianity are both considered Abrahamic religions and share common roots, their history has nevertheless been described primarily in terms of their conflicts. The Christian West never accepted the defeat of the Byzantine forces in 636 that led to the loss of Jerusalem and neighboring territories to Muslims. To many European Christians, this ongoing conflict was not merely over territorial expansion but over religious supremacy. They saw Christianity as being challenged by Islam, a religion whose followers believed it was the culmination of the Judeo-Christian tradition, and who believed that their sacred scripture, the Qur'an, was God's final revelation to humanity. Islam claimed to have a divine mandate to spread the word of God throughout the world, a claim that many Christians also considered their right.

By the eleventh century, at the request of Byzantine Emperor Alexis I and in response to a call by Pope Urban II, a huge army of Europeans started a drive ostensibly intended to end Muslim rule of Jerusalem. This campaign became known as the Crusades, a long-lasting series of bloody conflicts between Islamic and Christian European armies that took place between 1095 and 1453. The Christian forces were comprised of Roman Catholics, who actually considered the Byzantine Christians heretics and sacked Constantinople during the fourth major Crusade rather than proceeding on to Jerusalem.

The Christian armies captured Jerusalem from the Muslims in 1099 and held it for about ninety years, until 1187, when the Muslims regained control. Although the Christians never successfully retook Jerusalem, they made several additional attempts in further Crusades over the following centuries. The Crusades officially ended when the city of Constantinople, the capital of the Byzantine Empire, fell to the army of an Ottoman king during the mid-fifteenth century. The city was later renamed "Istanbul," and remained the seat of the Ottoman sultans until 1923. Muslims maintained a strong cultural presence on the Iberian Peninsula (present-day Spain and Portugal) from their first incursions in the early eighth century until the fall of the last Muslim kingdoms in 1492, the year the Spanish Inquisition began. Modern historical analyses of the Crusades indicate that these were primarily economic and strategic battles for control of trade routes and natural resources rather than strictly religious wars.

By the eighteenth century, when the Industrial Revolution provided an impetus for the expansion of European colonialism, the Islamic Middle East was long past its years of glory and had grown too weak to resist Western colonial ambitions. The Europeans' search for raw material and other economic resources enticed them to send armies all over the world, including into Islamic domains. Superior weapons and technology shifted the balance of power toward the European side. The Islamic world nearly succumbed to a Western power when Napoleon Bonaparte, then a young French general, successfully invaded Egypt in 1798. Later, the Ottoman sultans, who were the strongest remaining Islamic rulers, proved no match for the emerging Western powers. They lost their East European territories and most of their holdings in North Africa to various European forces. Similarly, the Mughal Empire that had ruled India for about four hundred years fell to the British in 1857. The Dutch colonized formerly Muslim-held regions of Southeast Asia. From Morocco to Malaysia, Muslims became the subjects of colonial powers. Faced with this turn of events, some pious Muslims felt that their destiny had been seized by foreigners and that God had abandoned them as punishment for their deviations from the true path of Islam.

Under the supervision of colonial powers (France, England, Holland, and Italy), the caliphates and sultanates that symbolically represented the Islamic system of authority were dismantled and replaced by new secular governments. European overlords created new countries and defined their borders, in many cases without any regard for physical or cultural criteria that had once shaped the territories. Often, they handpicked rulers for these countries from among their own loyal subjects and actively supported them throughout their reigns. The stability of these colonial governments depended upon foreign backing and a strong, loyal military rather than popular support won through elections or other democratic means.

The elite of these governments, along with some foreign-educated upper-class urbanites, promoted Western ideas, values, and culture in the newly colonized Muslim lands. Many Muslims gradually began to develop an appetite for the ways of the West, and the Westernization of Muslim societies soon became a widespread phenomenon. People developed a taste for Western clothing, art, architecture, literature, and particularly, forms of entertainment such as music and movies. To be modern it was considered necessary to adopt a European-American lifestyle.

In some countries, Westernization was imposed on Muslims by their government, not spontaneously chosen by the people. Kemal Ataturk of Turkey and Reza Shah of Iran during the first half of the twentieth century forced their subjects to follow the Western way of life by banning the wearing of traditional Islamic attire in public and by closing many Islamic madrasahs and replacing them with secular schools. Ataturk actually forced publishers and schools to use a modified Latin alphabet instead of the usual Turkish alphabet based on Arabic letterforms that had a strong symbolic link with the sacred language of the Qur'an. He dissolved the status of Islam as the official religion of Turkey, and replaced the shari'ah law courts with a new model based on European legal systems.

Most Islamic countries, including Egypt, Iraq, Syria, Pakistan, Malaysia, and Indonesia, adopted Western-style government, education, banking, and other institutions but attempted to retain their Islamic culture by preserving Muslim family law and supporting religious schools and institutions. The most heavily Westernized Islamic countries are those whose populations have had a high level of contact with the West, such as Turkey, Iran, Egypt, Lebanon, and Tunisia. The most traditional Muslim countries have been Saudi Arabia, Yemen, Oman, Afghanistan, and Pakistan.

THE ISLAMIC RESPONSE TO THE WEST

While the diffusion of Western science and technology into Muslim countries significantly improved physical infrastructures, it also introduced an ever-increasing appetite for material goods. Western reliance upon science and technology as the ultimate solutions to human problems began to undermine the prevailing Islamic worldview of the sovereignty of God and the need to observe ethical-religious codes of behavior as defined by shari'ah. For some people, materialism came to be seen as a way to satisfy sensual desires, regardless of the virtues recommended by Islam. Western music, television, and movies, as well as social mixing between the sexes, became widespread, and behaviors not traditionally common in Islamic societies, such as usury, alcohol consumption, prostitution, and pornography, also became more prevalent. Although these vices are universal problems, and not something strictly introduced by the West, for some religious groups in particular, contact with Europeans has been blamed as their cause. Western nations and Westernized rulers were held responsible for the breakdown of traditional family, religious, and social values; an increase in the divorce rate; and the overall moral decline of Islamic society.

Religious activists in many Muslim countries would like their governments to control the spread of Western values by being more selective in what is communicated through mass media. For example, they believe that the broadcasting of certain American television series, such as *Days of Our Lives*, *Dallas*, and *Dynasty*, contributes to the spread of promiscuous behavior and adultery among people whose faith is weak. Although these opposition groups may appreciate Western technology, they do not care for some aspects of Western culture. In other words, it might be said that they appreciate television, but not the apparent lack of values in the shows that are often broadcast. Some religious and social activists even believe that materialism and consumerism constitute a form of idolatry and have taught people to worship things instead of worshiping God.

The corruption of moral values through cross popular

entertainment has not occurred in Islamic cultures alone, nor has it been the sole factor contributing to the changes that have disturbed Islamic societies since the influx of Westernization. The colonial rulers failed to provide their subject populations with basic necessities such as employment opportunities, housing, food, and social-support systems. As a result, many Muslims believed that Western-style governments were incapable of responding adequately to the needs of Muslims.

Since the end of colonial rule in the twentieth century, Islamic countries, such as Egypt and Indonesia, have experimented with a variety of Western economic and governmental systems, including socialism, capitalism, and other secular forms; none has seemed to work. Under all of these systems, the gap between the wealthy few and the economically disenfranchised increased to the point where many people were reduced to living below the poverty line. Ironically, improvements such as better health care led to a significant reduction in death rates, but also caused rapid population increases (especially in rural regions). That population growth resulted in increased migrations to urban areas, where former rural residents added to the numbers of unemployed and dispossessed urban dwellers. In many cases, mass migrations from rural to urban regions led to the growth of vast shantytowns on the edge of major cities. In some cities, such as Cairo, the homeless have occupied cemeteries, calling them "Cities of Death."

In many former Muslim-ruled countries, the failure of governments to bring prosperity and stability to their nations has called the value of all Western systems into question. The legitimacy of these rulers and their dependency upon foreign aid and protection raised questions about national and cultural identity, sovereignty, and independence from superpowers. When capitalist and Communist nations were the staunchest of world rivals, some Muslim rulers took advantage of Western (especially American) opposition to communism in order to destroy legitimate dissent within their countries; they would foster opposition against dissenting groups by labeling them

Communists or Communist sympathizers. Muslim rulers used these tactics to dismantle political parties and organizations that were legitimately and democratically challenged their authoritarian rule. Throughout Muslim countries, an atmosphere of fear and mistrust of Western-supported, nondemocratic regimes empowered religious activists to organize their activities through mosques and religious centers where governmental forces could not stop them. Religious groups came to embody the main opposition to unpopular governments, and they recruited their members from among educated professionals and intellectuals and the economically disadvantaged. Many dissatisfied citizens, who were not religious but were concerned about a better future for their country, joined religious organizations in the struggle for political change. The power of these religious groups was clearly demonstrated in the process that led to the fall of the Shah of Iran and the emergence of the Islamic Republic of Iran in 1979.

THE ISLAMIC ALTERNATIVE

Western models of development have not worked well in Islamic countries. Modernization has become synonymous with Westernization, and Western cultural encroachments have resulted in disillusionment and an identity crisis for many Muslims. Once-independent Muslims with rich histories and strong cultural identities began to feel like the playthings of foreigners. Western models of development have tended to discount indigenous innovations that are not based on Western interests, and often, locally developed plans have tended to imitate Western models without respect for native cultural and natural circumstances. These trends have encouraged dependence on outsiders, and left the governments of Islamic nations serving outside interests instead of their own.

Many Muslim intellectuals have begun to notice that regional problems are more easily solved through local solutions. In a search to rediscover their unique identities and to reclaim their societies, many have felt that a return to Islamic ideals would be the best plan. They want to raise Muslims' shattered morale as individuals and as a community. They have begun to think of Islam not just as a religion but as an alternative to the seemingly relentless process of Europeanization or Americanization. These people seek to return to an Islamic lifestyle, as a replacement for what they perceive is the decadent Western lifestyle. They believe that the Qur'an and the sunnah of the Prophet should once again become the criteria for managing society, as they were during the time of Muhammad. Islam is again being perceived as a political force that is capable of correcting the wrongs of society.

The reemerging power of Islam caught the attention of some Muslim rulers and their Western allies during the second half of the twentieth century. They used this power to their advantage. Rulers such as Anwar Sadat of Egypt and Zia al-Haqq of Pakistan used Islam to legitimize their power among the populace. Western powers like the United States used religion-based groups such as the *mujahideen* of Afghanistan to fight the Soviet Union. The idea of building a "Green Belt" (green is the color most strongly identified with Islam) against communism became popular in the West, and served as a reason to support religious-minded people such as Zia al-Haqq against his socialist predecessor, Zulfikar Ali Bhutto in Pakistan.

The Islamic revival in many societies resulted in the establishment of many Islamic-inspired institutions, including mosques, schools, clinics, hospitals, day-care centers, youth centers, legal aid centers for the poor and for abused women, and financial institutions, such as interest-free Islamic banks. People from traditionally "nonreligious" sectors—businesspeople, lawyers, engineers, doctors, teachers, professors, bankers, military officers, and politicians—became Muslim activists. During the 1990s, Muslim political parties became very active and won seats in parliaments and other government offices in Egypt, Turkey, Algeria, Jordan, Malaysia, and Indonesia. In Turkey and Algeria, they even managed to defeat their opponents in national elections, and became majority political parties. The majority of Muslim activists are peaceful citizens who work within the context of legal political processes to attain their social and political goals. For example, Muslim activists have served as the prime minister of Turkey (arguably the most secular of Muslim countries) and as the president and speaker of the National Assembly in Indonesia, the largest Muslim nation.

ISLAMIC FUNDAMENTALISM

The term *fundamentalism* technically refers to a twentieth-century conservative American Protestant movement advocating a return to the basic beliefs and practices of Christianity, such as the virgin birth of Jesus, his physical resurrection, the infallibility of the Bible, Jesus's atonement for humanity's sins, and the expected second coming of Jesus. The movement also demanded, among other things, continued restrictions on women's reproductive choices, the disenfranchisement of homosexuals, and closer ties between the institutions of government and churches. Gradually, the term *fundamentalism* found a wider usage, being applied to any type of militant religious activity found in the world.

In Islamic societies where Islamic resurgence has become common, these movements are known as "revivalist" and "assertionist." In the West, the word *fundamentalist*, when referring to Muslims, is used loosely to describe a wide variety of Muslim activists who often have little in common, from the rulers of Iran to the members of al-Qaeda (the religio-political organization responsible for the 9/11 terrorist attack).

One of the early revivalists of modern times was Muhammad ibn Abd al-Wahhab (1703–1791), who launched a movement named after him (the "Wahhabis") on the Arabian Peninsula. The Wahhabi movement's fanatical approach to monotheism and its rejection of all religious symbols earned the Wahhabis the pejorative label "puritans," after the seventeenth-century group of Christians that originated in England but eventually immigrated to America to avoid religious persecution.

Abd al-Wahhab advocated what he called a "return" to an absolute form of Islam based upon the Qur'an and the sunnah of the Prophet that would theoretically purify Islam of all innovations (*bid'ah*) that had accrued since the death of Muhammad. Abd al-Wahhab enforced his "puritanical Islam" with the help of his collaborator and protector, the tribal chief ibn Sa'ud, whose children now rule Saudi Arabia, a country that was actually named after him. Abd al-Wahhab's early followers destroyed the shrines of Muhammad's familial descendants, the Shiite imams. They even removed the Prophet's tombstone, declaring it a sign of idolatry and intercession between God and humanity. (It is interesting to note that, in recent years, Mulla 'Umar, the head of the former Taliban government in Afghanistan, destroyed precious Buddhist monuments in Bamiyan based on the same argument.)

Today, Wahhabi Islam is the official form of Islam practiced in Saudi Arabia. One result of this is that Saudi Arabia has become the strictest Muslim country in regard to segregation of the sexes. According to the Wahhabis, Islam is the only way to salvation. Wahhabis are not known for their tolerance of other religions, and they regard even their fellow Muslims, if they are Shiites, as heretics and have actively persecuted them. The Saudi Arabian government has spent a generous amount of money to spread Wahhabi Islam throughout Afghanistan, Pakistan, the Central Asian republics, Southeast Asia, and even China, Europe, and the United States. There are also other movements that are similar to the Wahhabis, including the Salafiyyah of Syria and Egypt and the Muhammadiyyah of Indonesia.

Like the Wahhabis, the twentieth-century Islamic revolutionaries of Iran also wanted to create a Muhammadan Society (*Jame'eh Muhammadi*), returning the nation to the pristine Islam practiced at the time of the Prophet and applying shari'ah to all societal affairs. Although prior to the 1979 Iranian Revolution it was one of the most modern and Westernized Islamic countries, Iran now has a government that is as close as possible to a theocracy, a nation governed by religious leaders. Iran, in fact, may be the world's only theocracy. If *theocracy* means that religious clerics who claim to represent God's will rule a country, then Iran is without any doubt a theocracy. According to the founder of the Islamic

Revolution, Ayatollah Ruhollah Khomeini, sovereignty lies in the hands of God; rulers are merely instruments who implement the will of God through the application of shari'ah.

What makes the Iranian system interesting is that democratic governmental institutions, such as the office of president and a parliament, function alongside theocratic institutions such as the office of the Supreme Religious Leader (*Wali e Faqih*), the Assembly of Experts, and the Guardian Council. Although Iran is, in a sense, a limited democracy (the president and members of parliament are elected by popular vote), the democratic process provides no real power to elected officials. Actual political authority is wielded by the Supreme Religious Leader and members of the Guardian Council, who are not elected. Obviously, despite any claims to the contrary, it would be extraordinarily difficult for any government to embody the absolute will of God, and it is especially telling that the theocracy of Iran has fallen as far short of its declared ambitions, as have most other extreme religious movements.[16]

ISLAM AND TERRORISM

It is not difficult to understand the thinking of radical militant fundamentalists. Their worldview is often rooted in fears or suspicions that others want to destroy their preferred way of life. They often see the world in black-and-white terms, as a battle of good versus evil. They gather like-minded people around themselves to create a special enclave that segregates them from those they perceive as evildoers. Their laws are based upon fear and are strictly enforced by harsh punishments.

The Taliban of Afghanistan are a typical example of radical militant fundamentalists. They were brutally repressive toward their female population and those they considered their enemies. Unlike the average Muslim, who views God as merciful and compassionate, through the Qur'an and Islamic tradition, radical militant fundamentalists imagine God to be ferociously punitive and merciless. They tend to take on these cruel traits themselves. These groups are often as dangerous to their own members as they are to others, and are as capable of maintaining harsh interior discipline as they are of terrorizing those outsiders they consider their enemies. According to these radicals, the ends justify the means, and they insist on pursuing their political goals, even if innocent people are slaughtered in the process.

This attitude, fortunately, is not the norm. An average observant Muslim would prefer to effect social change by promoting religious ideals in a manner similar to the liberation theologies that are typically encountered in oppressed countries of the world. A tradition found in three books of ahadith defines a Muslim as "one from whose hands and tongue people are secure." According to another tradition, a *mu'min* (believer) is "One from whom people are secure concerning their lives and properties." The first verse revealed to Muhammad about war called for Muslims to defend themselves only under certain circumstances: "Permission to take up arms is hereby given to those who are attacked, because they have been wronged. God has power to grant victory to those who have been unjustly driven from their homes, only because they said 'Our Lord is God' . . ." (Q. 22:39–40). In another passage, God makes certain that Muslims should not be aggressive in war: "And fight in the way of God against those who fight against you, but be not aggressive, surely God loves not the aggressors" (Q. 2:190).

Individuals and groups who seek to accomplish their various goals have politicized Islam. Some political groups seeking to resist oppression and domination by internal or external sources find it easy to recruit sympathizers under the banner of religion, as the Christian Crusaders did in Europe during the Middle Ages. They are well aware of the power of religious sentiments and they tend to harness it to advance their own interests. Any observer of recent international political events might well ask if Islam encourages hatred of the wealthiest and most powerful Western nation, the United States. The answer is no—nothing in the religion of Islam does so. Neither the estimated 6 million Muslims who are loyal U.S. citizens nor most other Muslims around the world hate America. So, it is worth pondering why exactly the United States has become such a desirable target for terrorism, as in the case of the September 11, 2001, attacks on the Pentagon and the World Trade Center.

Most Muslims—the vast majority—throughout the world were appalled by the murder of innocents and asserted that there could be no legitimate justification within Islam for such a hideous act. At the same time, however, Muslims in the Middle East understood the attack as a political expression in response to what many see as an ill-conceived American foreign policy of fierce and uncompromising support for Israel that has been imposed upon the eastern Mediterranean region. Terrorism is usually the most extreme of the responses employed by those who have endured injustice and oppression, and who are frustrated because they see few ways to attract attention to their genuine grievances.

The terrorists of the eastern Mediterranean would doubtless prefer that the American government reevaluate its policies concerning the region, for example, by showing fairer treatment to the Muslim and Christian natives of Israel-Palestine. Terrorism is best viewed not as an unreasonable exercise of force but as a symptom of a larger "disease" whose roots deserve profound examination and reasoned treatment. Common sense should inform average Americans that they, like some Muslims in the Middle East, would be outraged if a wealthy powerful country on the other side of the world imposed its own political will upon them. Still, it is often difficult to understand the use of terror to achieve political goals.

Perhaps the most poorly understood tactics of "terrorism" have been the use of suicide bombers. Nothing in Islam encourages or justifies suicide for any reason; in fact, suicide is held to be among the gravest of sins. Suicide in Islam is the equivalent of murder, or perhaps even worse, because it denies the reality that God's will should prevail. In Islam, it is God alone who gives life and takes it away. A passage in the Qur'an indicates that killing an innocent person is like killing all of humanity, an enormous sin (Q. 5:32).

It is not Islam that inspires an individual to waste his or her precious life to prove a point. Suicide bombing is the last of all possible resorts and constitutes an act of extreme desperation. It may confirm the prejudices of one religious bigot to assert that another's religion advocates even suicide in pursuit of a religious cause. But to examine the matter with even a modicum of gravity, one must admit that others can be pushed to such an extreme expression of despair only by repeated and prolonged intense oppression, by which they are made to feel no alternative is possible except death. The causes of such frustration are obvious. It is worth examining other instances of suicide bombing and self-destruction, including the Tamils (Hindus) who wanted independence from the Sinhalese (Buddhists) on the island of Sri Lanka, or the Buddhist monks who immolated themselves in protest against the Nhu regime of Vietnam.

MUSLIMS IN THE WEST

One might ask, if Muslims in Islamic countries are so critical of Western culture and way of life, then why are so many Muslims living in Europe and the United States, and why are so many more willing or even eager to immigrate to the West? The issue can be addressed from several perspectives.

First, not every Muslim is an observant Muslim, just as every Christian is not an observant Christian. Interiorization and personalization of religion and even secularism are now a way of life for many people throughout the Islamic world, as elsewhere, and Islam has become for many Muslims a ritualistic observance instead of a valid religion. For example, many people of Persian heritage use their Qur'an only once a year during the celebration of the Iranian New Year (Norooz). Even then, it is often little more than a decorative item to fulfill the required rituals of the holiday. Westerners demonstrate wisdom by acknowledging that not every action taken by a so-called Muslim is actually Islamic. By parallel example, Muslims do not blame the criminal behavior of an American convict who happens to call him- or herself a Christian on the teachings of Christianity. Muslims would appreciate application of a similar attitude by Westerners that criminal acts committed by self-labeled Muslims are not representative of Islam. A terrorist who calls himself or herself a Muslim is just a terrorist, not an "Islamic" terrorist, even if he or she presents some clouded misunderstanding of his or her religion to justify an aberrant act. The mass media often sensationalize events by inflaming prejudices. These days in America, one does not usually read in a newspaper or see in a news report the religious identities of those who commit crimes unless they are self-proclaimed Muslims.

Second, Muslims do not oppose everything that the West stands for. Muslims appreciate the rule of law, respect for human rights, democracy, adequate social services, freedom of religious expression and the other freedoms guaranteed by the U.S. Constitution, a relatively low degree of corruption among government officials, and more sophisticated technology and science. They appreciate the respect for cultural diversity found in America and enjoy being able to practice their religion without harassment (at least most of the time).

To speak practically, the third and most important reason that Muslims immigrate to the West is probably increased access to economic opportunities compared to their home countries, which may be limited unless they belong to the ruling elite of their nation of origin.

Muslims have been in Europe since the eighth century when they established their rule in Spain, making Córdoba their capital. However, in modern times, the largest wave of Muslim immigration occurred during the post–World War II period, and again after the decolonization of Muslim countries in the later twentieth century. Many people from former European colonies immigrated to the countries of their colonizers. For example, there was a huge migration of Muslims from the South Asian subcontinent (Pakistan, India, Kashmir, and Bangladesh) to England, while a sizable number of North Africans moved to their former colonizer, France. Germany has also attracted a large number of Turkish immigrants due to long-standing relation-ships between Turkey and Germany. There are also Muslim immigrants in Belgium, Spain, the Netherlands, Sweden, Denmark, Norway, Austria, Bosnia, and Albania. Because of economic recessions and—to some extent—recent violent events in the Middle East, European countries today do not accept as many Muslim immigrants as they have done in the past.

MUSLIMS IN THE UNITED STATES

Although Canada has accepted many Muslims during the last decade, the majority of Muslims in North America live in the United States. There are many estimates of the number of Muslims in America, ranging anywhere from 4 to 12 million. The number upon which most scholars agree is 6 million.

Muslims are found in all major American cities; the largest Muslim communities are in New York City, Boston, Detroit, Chicago, Houston, Los Angeles, and Dearborn, Michigan. No other country in the world holds as diverse a Muslim population as that of the United States. America's Muslims come from Thailand, Malaysia, Indonesia, India, Bangladesh, Pakistan, Afghanistan, Iran, Iraq, Turkey, Lebanon, Syria, Jordan, Palestine, Egypt, Algeria, Morocco, Trinidad, Venezuela, and other parts of the world. The Friday noon communal prayer at the Muslim Community Center of Portland, Oregon, is a truly international experience in which Muslims from many different racial and ethnic backgrounds all take part.

The first Muslims to come to America were probably the Mudejars (Muslims living under Christian rule) and Moriscos (Spanish Muslims who converted to Christianity) among the Spanish explorers who sailed to the Western Hemisphere. However, a good portion (14 to 20 percent) of black slaves brought to America between the sixteenth and nineteenth centuries were Muslims, too. Since they were not allowed to practice their religion under the authority of their Christian masters, many of them were not able to transmit their religion to their descendants. Today, however, Muslims of African descent form about one-third of the Muslim population of the United States, with the other two-thirds being Muslim immigrants and

(continued on page 156)

THE ISLAMIC COMMUNITY CENTER
OF PORTLAND OREGON (*www.metpdx.org*)

Known as the Muslim Educational Trust (MET), the Islamic Community Center of Portland is located in a serene southwest neighborhood surrounded by tall trees. As a nonprofit organization, it was established in 1993 to serve the educational and social needs of Portland's growing Muslim community. MET's mission is to provide information about Islam to both Muslims and non-Muslims, to enrich the public's understanding of Islam, and to dispel common myths and stereotypes about Islam. It seeks to serve the Muslim community's educational needs and help develop new generations of well-adjusted, committed Muslims who are capable of facing the challenges of modern life with pride, dignity, and confidence in the Islamic path. MET is focused on Islam as a faith, a moral code, and a way of life. As the voice of Portland's Muslim community, MET is very active with the Islamic Social Service of Oregon State (ISOS) *www.i-sos.org* in helping Muslim immigrants and refugees settle in Portland area, and serves as an official local resource for Muslim visitors to the city. MET maintains a large library of books,

A non-pretentious building, the Islamic Community Center of Portland is located in a quiet neighborhood surrounded by tall trees.

pamphlets, audiotapes, and videos on Islam and the Muslim world and makes these available to the Muslim community, schools, and the public at large.

The center's outreach efforts include:

- Advocacy among local news organizations for non-biased news coverage.

- Workshops for teachers in the public school system.

.• Establishing links with other faiths that are opening channels for communication.

Islamic Community Center of Portland also serves as an educational institution. Here, at the request of the author, a group of students and teachers posed for a picture in the courtyard of the center.

- Presenting public lectures featuring prominent national and international scholars who are of relevance to both Muslims and non-Muslims.

- Presenting the loving and open face of Islam to a fearful American public.

- Cooperating with other organizations that serve the interests of Islam and Muslims.

Educating the children about Islam and Muslim rituals is one of the main goals of the center. Here, a teacher is teaching the ritual of Muslim daily prayers (*salat*) to a group of students. The calligraphy on the wall is a gift from Chinese Muslims to the center; it illustrates the declaration of faith (*shahadah*) in Islam in both Chinese and Arabic: "There is no deity but God; Muhammad is the Messenger of God."

- Serving as a liaison between Muslim organizations, Islamic centers, and the community.

- Operating an informal speaker's bureau of Muslims to speak at public schools and other interested groups, including churches.

- Publishing a quarterly newsletter, *Al-Hewar* (*The Dialogue*).

- Operating a full-time school, Islamic school of MET (ISMET), Pre-K, grades K–8 (a grade is added every year).

- Operating a weekend Islamic school. MET's Weekend School offers classes in Qur'an reading and memorization, Arabic and Islamic studies and history.

- Operating a summer day camp.

The center currently has more than seventy students enrolled. The diversity of students in this classroom exemplifies the overall ethnic diversity of Portland's Muslim population.

(*continued from page 151*)

their children, along with Americans of European descent who have embraced Islam. Muslims occupy all kinds of positions in the United States. Many Muslim immigrants are professionals who either received their academic degrees from American universities and decided to remain, or, like many Indians and Pakistanis, came to the United States to work as physicians, computer scientists, and in other professions.

Like Muslims in Europe, American Muslims are profoundly disturbed by the events of the Middle East, and they have occasionally faced mistreatment at the hands of overzealous and ignorant individuals. In response to harassment, many Muslims in America have adopted a strategy of keeping a low profile. Just as many, however, have decided to stand up as proud examples of the finest characteristics of their religion: It is not unusual to encounter Muslims who were not especially observant of their religion when they lived in their country of origin, but who have decided that America's climate of relative religious freedom enables them to practice their religion openly.

AFRICAN-AMERICAN ISLAM

African-American Islam has gone through many changes since its inception in the early twentieth century. The 1930s were a decade of economic hardship and depression for just about everyone, and doubtless were even harder to endure for descendants of African slaves, who were treated as second-class citizens in the United States.

Into this environment, a man who called himself Wallace D. Fard Muhammad appeared. He may have been a follower of an earlier African-American neo-Muslim named Noble Drew Ali, and he called himself the *Mahdi*, or "messiah," in the ghettos of Detroit. He started to promote Islam among the economically disenfranchised black population. The Islam he espoused was remote from orthodox Islam. Using both the Bible and the Qur'an for his preaching, he called his version of Islam the "religion of the black man" and emphasized the need to form a "Nation of Islam" that would separate blacks from prejudiced white Americans. He called for the self-removal of blacks from the economic system of a country that, in his view, was run by what he called the "blue-eyed devil."

Wallace Fard Muhammad's message of solidarity among blacks and avoidance of Christianity, which was seen as the religion of their oppressors, attracted some followers. Fard mysteriously disappeared, but in 1934, a man by the name of Elijah Muhammad (1897–1975), formerly known as Elihah Poole, appeared and took over the so-called Nation of Islam based on the teachings of Fard Muhammad. He called himself a prophet and taught that Fard had been divine. Both of these claims are considered forms of the worst possible sin (shirk) in Islam, since they assign a partner to God and call someone besides Muhammad the last messenger of God.

Elijah Muhammad was more of a Black Nationalist than an Islamic scholar. He contended that poverty, dependency, and self-hatred among African Americans were the consequences of oppression at the hands of whites. He heralded the fall of white racist America and the restoration of blacks as "chosen people." Through his teachings, he significantly elevated the self-esteem of his followers. He emphasized the "do it yourself" concept and focused on black pride and identity, which he believed were lacking among blacks. He also advocated other characteristics such as self-sufficiency, strong family values, hard work, discipline, physical strength, and the avoidance of alcohol, gambling, and drugs.

The Nation of Islam had a membership of about 100,000 by the 1970s, and it became financially self-sufficient. It owned a substantial amount of real estate, including hundreds of temples and businesses.

After the death of Elijah in 1975, his son Wallace implemented major reforms in conformity with orthodox Sunni Islam. He opened membership to people of all races, and stopped calling whites the "blue-eyed devil." Under his influence, Wallace Fard came to be considered the founder of the Nation of Islam rather than a god, and Elijah was viewed as the first leader of the Nation instead of a prophet. As in traditional Islam, temples were called mosques and ministers were called imams. Members observed the Five Pillars, and the push for separation from the rest of the country ended. Members were encouraged instead to become responsible U.S. citizens. In the mid-1980s, Wallace chose an Islamic name, calling himself Warith Deen Muhammad. He also renamed his spiritual organization the American Muslim Mission, which was well-integrated with other Muslim groups throughout the world.

After the death of Elijah, in 1977, a faction under the leadership of Louis Farrakhan split from the main community (then headed by Wallace) and decided to preserve the Nation of Islam as it had been under Elijah. Farrakhan, a charismatic figure, has since attracted a lot of attention from the mass media—to the extent that many Americans do not realize that his group represents only a very small portion of black Muslims in the

MALCOLM X AND THE NATION OF ISLAM

Elijah Muhammad recruited new members from black ghettos and prisons. One of his greatest recruits was Malcolm X (formerly Malcolm Little), who accepted Islam while imprisoned for burglary and, when released, became the first minister of the Nation. Malcolm X was a gifted speaker and organizer. During his ministry, membership grew significantly. He managed to recruit people to the Nation of Islam, including the famous boxer Cassius Clay, who later became known as Muhammad Ali. Malcolm X was an intelligent man, and over time, he began to question the teachings of the Nation of Islam organization. Then, he made his life-changing pilgrimage to Mecca, where he met blue-eyed and blond-haired Muslims, pious people who were far from being "devils," as the Nation referred to whites. Upon his return to the United States, he changed his name to El-Hajj Malik El-Shabazz, a traditional Muslim name. He began preaching authentic Islam instead of the creed he had learned from Elijah Muhammad. He had a major influence on Elijah's son Wallace D. Muhammad, who is now the spiritual leader of the Black Muslims, a separate group from the Nation of Islam, and which follows orthodox Islam, unlike the Nation of Islam, which is considered heretical by worldwide Islam. Malcolm X was assassinated in a temple in New York City in 1965.

Source: Malcolm X and Alex Haley, *The Autobiography of Malcolm X*, New York: Ballantine Books, 1992.

United States. Farrakhan, however, has recently mellowed his rhetoric and has brought the Nation closer to traditional Islam.

ISLAM AND THE CHALLENGES OF GLOBALIZATION

If globalization means finding common ground through a free flow of goods and the exchange of economic, social, scientific, technological, and political benefits, as well as narrowing the gaps that separate diverse world communities, then Islam is not alien to the concept. For centuries, people from different regions of the world with widely varied ethnic and religious backgrounds have worked together to build a flourishing Islamic community. For example, in the years after the prophet Muhammad's death, the emerging Islamic powers borrowed ideas from the Persians to construct their governing system and utilized ideas from the Romans to build their defense and security system. They also employed the philosophical knowledge of legendary Greek figures such as Plato and Aristotle to build a bridge between faith and reason. Today, the majority of Muslims would like to establish such a common ground by which less-developed nations can benefit and prosper from contact with more advanced nations without fear of being politically, economically, or culturally dominated.

Today's Muslim response to globalization is expressed by different voices with distinct concerns. This is because Islam is not monolithic. More than 1.2 billion Muslims inhabit this Earth, and it is unrealistic to expect all of them to react to changing global conditions in the same way. One thing is obvious: The extremists and radicals whose response to increasing globalization is isolationism are not the Muslim majority. They are a small group of people who are unhappy with the current direction of the world political economy, and are reacting to what they perceive as a massive injustice. These extremists perceive globalization as nothing less than Western domination of the world; they see the trend as a continuation of what they once called colonialism and imperialism.

Unlike these people, the bulk of the world's Muslim population has no interest in isolationism. Rather, they would like to participate actively in world affairs. Their approach to politics is not very different from that of Christians. They believe that Islam should not be politicized because a politicized Islam would overshadow the religion's spiritual dimension, in which a majority of Muslims are much more interested.

With a higher literacy rate and increased levels of education, Muslims today study their religion more critically than ever before. They tend to look for aspects of the message of Islam that help them with their personal life and spiritual maturity. Intellectual Muslims are critical of reading narrations related to Muhammad and they study shari'ah, the Islamic law, more carefully and analytically than did Muslims of past days. Currently, Muslim scholars are debating whether all shari'ah laws (which were put into effect during the early centuries of Islam) are still applicable today. Some even question the relevance of certain Qur'anic verses from Muhammad's period in Medina, since they were revealed at a time when Muhammad was building the first Muslim community. They were appropriate in the sociopolitical conditions of Medina, but may perhaps be less so in the situations Muslims face in modern life. In contrast, Muslim intellectuals emphasize the universal applicability of the Meccan verses, due to their religious, rather than politically oriented, nature.

Muslim nations also have been criticized for the treatment of their female populations. Although Islamic countries during recent decades have had several female heads of states (i.e., Tanzu Ciller in Turkey, Benazir Bhutto in Pakistan, and Khaleda Zia in Bangladesh) and many women ministers, judges, and members of parliament, the treatment of women in some Muslim countries still needs improvement. Perhaps the area that needs the most modernization is family law, with regard to marriage, divorce, and inheritance. Employment and educational opportunities outside the home for women who are willing to learn and work must also be expanded. Of course, a vast body of literature has been published about the status of women in Islam, much of it written by Muslim female scholars. Analysts often argue that the position of women as advocated by the Qur'an is much more humane in theory than it is in practice, and that cultural practices have obscured the authentic intention of Islam, with one result being that women have been relegated to second-class status.

Fortunately, Islam does provide a solution for fixing many emerging legal problems through thoughtful utilization of *ijtihad*, or critical individual reasoning. Ijtihad is an important component of Islamic law. If Islam intends to serve humanity for another millennium, it needs to make proper use of ijtihad and apply ijtihad wisely and productively to changing circumstances that arise in different times and places. It took a group of brilliant scholars nearly a hundred years between the ninth and tenth centuries to write the current laws. What is needed now is another major project in which students of Islamic jurisprudence would use their knowledge of Islam, combined with the application of common sense, to make shari'ah more applicable to this modern age without compromising the principal ideals of Islam.

Another challenge to Muslim communities in this age of globalization is to uphold the human rights of non-Muslims who live in Muslim countries. Now that all world nations have become more multicultural, Muslim countries cannot continue to regard their non-Muslim populations as second-class citizens. Just as Muslims living in non-Muslim countries demand equal treatment, likewise, Muslim countries need to provide a social environment in which people who uphold right conduct regardless of their religious practices are appreciated and accepted as equals. People should not be punished simply because their understanding of monotheism differs from that of the Islamic community. Monotheism, after all, does not mean monolithic. Now more than ever, Muslims need to remember that God, Most Merciful and Most Compassionate, does not discriminate between members of the human race:

> O Humankind, We have created you from a male and female, and formed you into nations and tribes that you may know each other. The noblest of you in the sight of God is the best in conduct. God is All-knowing and Well-informed (Q. 49:13).

570 Muhammad, the son of Abdullah and Aminah, is born in Mecca

610 Muhammad receives the first revelation through the archangel Gabriel while meditating in a cave outside Mecca

622 Muhammad leaves Mecca for Medina

630 Muhammad's followers capture Mecca and destroy the idols in the Kaaba

632 Muhammad dies in Medina

632–661 Orthodox caliphate of the Four Rightly Guided Caliphs (in Mecca and Medina)

632–634 Abu Bakr serves as the first caliph

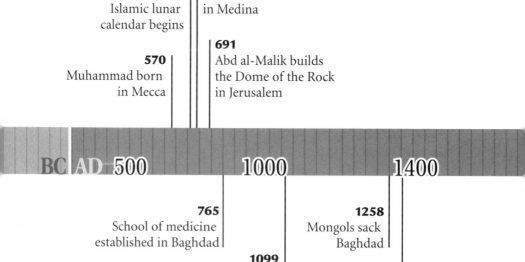

622
The Year of Hijrah;
Islamic lunar
calendar begins

632
Muhammad dies
in Medina

691
Abd al-Malik builds
the Dome of the Rock
in Jerusalem

570
Muhammad born
in Mecca

BC AD 500 **1000** **1400**

765
School of medicine
established in Baghdad

1258
Mongols sack
Baghdad

1099
Crusaders take
Jerusalem

1389
Ottomans defeat
Serbs at Kosovo

634-644   Umar serves as second caliph

636   Muslims defeat the Byzantine Empire and take control of Syria

637   Muslims defeat the Persian Sassanid Empire

638   Muslims annex Jerusalem as an Islamic city

641   Muslims conquer Alexandria, Egypt

644-656   'Uthman serves as third caliph; the official text of the Qur'an is compiled

656-661   'Ali serves as fourth caliph; in a civil war, the Umayyads challenge the caliphate of 'Ali

661   'Ali dies

1798–1799
Napoleon Bonaparte
tries to conquer Egypt

1924
Office of
caliph abolished

1914
Ottoman Empire
enters World War I as
one of the Central Powers

1800

1900

2000

1948
The state of Israel created;
Arab armies defeated
in a war with Israel

1979
Iran becomes an
Islamic republic

CHRONOLOGY

661–750	Mu'awiya establishes the Umayyad Caliphate; the capital is transferred from Medina to Damascus
680	Mu'awiya dies and his son Yazid succeeds him; Husayn Ali's son and his followers rebel against Yazid and are massacred in Karbala in present-day Iraq
685–687	Shiite revolt takes place in Iraq
711	Muslims expand their rule to Spain
750–1258	Abbasid Caliphate replaces Umayyads with the help of Shiite Persian General Abu Muslim; capital is transferred to Baghdad
756–1031	Umayyad emirate in Spain, with the capital at Córdoba
910–1171	Fatimid Caliphate in Egypt, with the capital at Cairo
1095–1099	First Crusade
1147–1149	Second Crusade
1187	Saladin recaptures Jerusalem from the Crusaders and civilians are spared
1189–1192	Third Crusade
1350–1918	The Ottoman Empire
1379–1401	Tamerlane establishes an empire in Persia, Iraq, and Syria
1453	Constantinople is conquered; city renamed Istanbul
1483–1857	Mughal Empire in India
1501–1723	Safavid Empire in Persia
1501	Ismail becomes shah of Persia, founding the Safavid Empire; Shiism becomes the official religion
1520–1566	Suleiman II the Magnificent

1587–1629 Reign of Shah Abbas I

1703 Muhammad Abd al-Wahhab, the founder of Wahhabi Islam, is born

1811 Ali Muhammad Bab, the founder of Babi movement that leads to the formation of the Baha'i movement, is born

1882 Egypt comes under British military occupation

1905 The revivalist Salafiyyah movement starts in Paris with its main influence in Egypt

1912 The revivalist Muhammadiyyah movement starts in Indonesia

1914 The Ottoman Empire enters World War I as one of the Central Powers

1919–1924 End of the Ottoman Empire

1928 Turkey is declared a secular state; Hasan al-Banna founds the Muslim Brotherhood in Egypt

1935 Iran becomes the official name of Persia

1948 The state of Israel is created; Arab armies are defeated in a war with Israel

1968 The enlargement plan of Kaaba the mosque in Mecca is completed

1975 Wallace (Warith Deen) Muhammad assumes leadership of Nation of Islam in the United States and shifts movement toward Islamic orthodoxy, renaming it American Muslim Mission

1979 Iran becomes an Islamic republic

NOTES

Chapter 2: Muhammad

1 This sermon can be viewed online at Islamic Server of MSA-USC: *http://www.usc.edu/dept/MSA/*.

Chapter 4: Worldview

2 Babak Ayazifar, "Intellect and Reason in the Islamic Worldview," *The Tech*, Vol. 121, No. 51, 2001. Available online at *http://www-tech.mit.edu/V121/N51/col51babak.51c.html*.

Chapter 5: Worship

3 For a more detailed description of mosques and other religious structures of Muslim Iranian cities, see my discussion of religion and sociopolitical structures in *Iranian Cities: Formation and Development*, Syracuse University Press, 2000.

Chapter 7: Cultural Expressions

4 Rabi'ah al-Adawiyya, trans. Andrew Harvey and Eryk Hanut, *Perfume of the Desert*, Quest Books, 1999.

5 Ibn al-'Arabi, "Tarjuman al-Ashwaq," *The Mystics of Islam*, trans. Reynold A. Nicholson, World Wisdom Books, 2002.

6 Shaikh Abu Saeed Abil Kheir, *Nobody, Son of Nobody*, Hohm Press, 2001.

7 Ibn al-'Arabi, "Tarjuman al-Ashwaq," *The Mystics of Islam*, trans. Reynold A. Nicholson, World Wisdom Books, 2002.

8 Available online at University of North Carolina at Wilmington, "Samples of Sufi Writings," *http://people.uncw.edu/bergh/par230/L39RSufi.htm*.

9 Abu Hamid al-Ghazali, "Munkidh min al-Dalal (*Confessions*, or *Deliverance from Error*)," *Internet Medieval Sourcebook*. Available online at *http://www.fordham.edu/halsall/basis/1100ghazali-truth.html*.

10 For a detailed study of science and technology in Islam, see Al-Hassan Ahmad and Donald Hill, *Islamic Technology: An Illustrated History*, Cambridge University Press, 1994.

11 George Sarton, "Introduction to the History of Science, Vol. I–IV," Carnegie Institute of Washington, Baltimore, 1927–1931.

Chapter 8: Holidays

12 For date conversions between the two calendars, visit the Gregorian-Hijri date converter online at *http://www.rabiah.com/convert/convert.php3*.

13 For a lively discussion of this and other Muslim holidays, see Ann Marie Bahr's articles published in *The Brookings Register* (March 25, 1999; December 9, 1999; April 6, 2000; May 11, 2000; June 15, 2000; December 13, 2001; and March 7, 2002).

Chapter 9: Memories

14 The term *fundamentalism* is used very loosely here, since there is no such concept as "fundamentalism" in Islam.

15 Sir John Bagot Glubb, *A Short History of the Arab Peoples*. Quotation available online at *http://cyberistan.org/islamic/quote2.html*.

Chapter 10: Islam in the World Today

16 For more information about the structure of the post-revolutionary Iranian government, see Masoud Kheirabadi, *Modern World Nations: Iran*, Chelsea House Publishers, 2003.

BOOKS

Al-Hassan, Ahmad, and Donald Hill. *Islamic Technology: An Illustrated History.* Cambridge University Press, 1994.

Ali, Ahmad. *Al-Qur'an: A Contemporary Translation.* Princeton University Press, 1993.

Dawood, N.J. *The Koran.* Penguin Books, 1990.

Denny, Frederick. *Islam.* Harper San Francisco, 1987.

Esposito, John. *Islam: The Straight Path.* Oxford University Press, 1998.

Kheirabadi, Masoud. *Iranian Cities: Formation and Development.* Syracuse University Press, 2000.

———. *Modern World Nations: Iran.* Chelsea House Publishers, 2003.

Maududi, Sayyid Abul A'la. *Towards Understanding Islam,* trans. and ed. Khurshid Ahmad. 8th ed. Islamic Teaching Center, 1988.

Nasr, Seyyed Hossein. *Islam: Religion, History, and Civilization.* Harper San Francisco, 2003.

Oxtoby, Williard G. *World Religions: Western Traditions.* 2nd ed. Oxford University Press, 2002.

Robinson, Francis, ed. *Cambridge Illustrated History: Islamic World.* Cambridge University Press, 1998.

Yusufali, Abdullah. *The Holy Qur'an: Text, Translation and Commentary.* Tahrike Tarsile Qur'an, Inc., 1988.

WEBSITES

Amnesty International
http://www.bartleby.com/65/ir/Iran.html

Columbia Encyclopedia
http://www.bartleby.com/65/ir/Iran.html

BIBLIOGRAPHY

Country Analysis Brief
  http://www.mideastinfo.com/iran.htm

Internet History Sourcebooks Project
  http://www.fordham.edu/halsall/

Introduction to Islam by M. Cherif Bassiouini
  http://www2.ari.net/gckl/islam/titlepage.htm

Islamic Center of Greater Toledo
  http://www.icgt.org/

Islamic Civilization
  http://www.cyberistan.org/

Islamic Republic of Iran
  http://www.mideastinfo.com/iran.htm

Islamic Server of MSA-USC
  http://www.usc.edu/dept/MSA/

Ismaeli Website
  http://www.amaana.org/ismaili.html

Mage Publishers Inc.
  http://www.mage.com/TLbody.html

The National Iranian American Council
  http://cyberiran.com/history/

Nuradeen
  http://www.nuradeen.com/nuradeen.htm

"Recent Changes and Future of Fertility in Iran"
  by Mohammad Jalal Abbasi Shavazi
  http://www.un.org/esa/population/publications/
  completingfertility/ABBASIpaper.PDF

Statistical Center of Iran
  http://www.unescap.org/pop/popin/profiles/iran/popin2.htm

Statistical, economic and social research and training center
  for Islamic countries
  http://www.sesrtcic.org/defaulteng.shtml

PRIMARY SOURCES

Al-Bukhari, Muhammad Ibn Ismaiel, *Sahih al-Bukhari: The Translation of the Meanings 9 Vol. Set*, trans. Mohammad M. Khan. Darussalam, 1997.

Ali, Ahmad. *Al-Qur'an: A Contemporary Translation*. Princeton University Press, 1993.

Cleaey, Thomas, et al. *The Wisdom of the Prophet: The Sayings of Muhammad*. Shambhala Publications, 2001.

Dawood, N.J. *The Koran*. Penguin Books, 1990.

Yusufali, Abdullah. *The Holy Qur'an: Text, Translation and Commentary*. Tahrike Tarsile Qur'an, Inc., 1988.

SECONDARY SOURCES

Armstrong, Karen. *The Battle for God*. Knopf, 2000.

Esposito, John, and Natana J. DeLong-Bas. *Women in Muslim Family Law (Contemporary Issues in the Middle East)*. Syracuse University Press, 2002.

Gragg, Kenneth. *Jesus and the Muslim: An Exploration*. Oneworld Publications,1999.

Hodgson, Marshall. *Venture of Islam: Conscience and History in a World Civilization: The Expansion of Islam in the Middle Periods*. University of Chicago Press, 1977.

Leaman, Oliver. *An Introduction to Classical Islamic Philosophy*. Cambridge University Press, 2002.

Nasr, S.H. *Sufi Essays*. Library of Islam Ltd., 1999.

Wadud, Amina. *Qur'an and Woman: Rereading the Sacred Text from a Woman's Perspective*. Oxford University Press, 1999.

Watt, Montgomery. *A Short History of Islam*. Oneworld Publications, 1996.

FURTHER READING

WEBSITES

Internet History Sourcebooks Project

http://www.fordham.edu/halsall/

An extensive collection of primary and secondary sources on all aspects of world history from ancient times through the modern day.

Islamic Center of Greater Toledo

http://www.icgt.org/

A local institution in the Toledo area, it offers general information on Islam in the interests of helping to educate the American public.

Islamic Civilization

http://www.cyberistan.org/

Provides a wide variety of information on Islamic history, including extensive biographical data about Muhammad.

Islamic Republic of Iran

http://www.mideastinfo.com/iran.htm

An Iran-based site, offers historical, political, and cultural information about Iran, as well as links to Iranian newspapers and other sites of interest.

Islamic Server of MSA-USC

http://www.usc.edu/dept/MSA/

The official site of the Muslim Students Association at the University of Southern California; provides pertinent information for both Muslim and non-Muslim readers seeking to research the history and culture of Islam.

INDEX

Europe
  and colonialism, 138-139, 141
  Islam in, 8, 16, 149-151.
  See also West
Eve, 5, 48-49, 85
extremist Islam. *See* Islamic fundamentalism

faith
  declaration of. *See shahadah*
  deep personal, 80
  and Muhammad, 78-79
  and reason, 93-94
family, and pre-Islamic Arabia, 20
faqir (poor), 96.
  See also Sufism
Fard, Wallace, 157-158
Farrakhan, Louis, 158-159
fasting during Ramadan. *See saum*
Fatamid, 101
fath (military conquest), 121-124
Fatimah, 23
Festival of Breaking the Fast. *See*
  Id al-Fitr
Festival of Sacrifice. *See Id al-Adha*
festivals. *See* holidays; *id (eid)*
fitrah (sound nature), 44, 48, 49, 80
Five Pillars of Islam, 61, 63, 79-85
  almsgiving, 29, 61, 63, 75, 76, 79,
    80-81, 122
  declaration of faith, 61, 63, 79-80
  fasting during Ramadan, 29, 61,
    63, 79, 81-83, 115-116
  pilgrimage to Mecca, 21, 27, 29, 61,
    63, 79, 83-85
  prayers. *See salat*
Four Rightly Guided Caliphs, 125-127
France, Islam in, 16, 150
Friday, and communal prayers,
  65-67, 68
Friday mosque *(Masjid al-Jum'ah)*,
  66-67, 68
fundamentalism, 144.
  See also Islamic fundamentalism
funerals, 78

Gabriel *(Jibril)*, 23-24, 32, 33, 34, 43,
  54, 113, 115, 118
gender
  and Saudi Arabia, 145
  and weddings, 77-78.
  See also women
geography, 106
Germany, Islam in, 16, 150
Ghadir Khumm, 125-126
ghusl (complete ablution), 65
globalization, and Islam, 159-165
God (Allah), 50
  as forgiving and merciful, 51-52
  and humankind as vicegerent,
    46-48
  and human rights of non-Muslims,
    161
  and monotheism, 4, 6, 50-53, 57
  Muhammad as messenger of,
    23-24, 27, 30, 37-38, 79, 80
  and Qur'an, 4, 7, 33-34, 35, 36-38,
    39, 51
  and revelations to Muhammad,
    23-24
  and spread of Islam, 121
  submission to, 3, 37, 49, 52-53,
    61, 62-63, 79, 80. *See also* Five
    Pillars of Islam
golden age. *See* cultural expressions
Gospel, 7, 35, 36, 56
government
  and Abbasids, 132
  and almsgiving, 80-81
  and Iran, 142, 145-146
  and Islamic community, 124-125
  and mosques, 68
  and Muslim activists, 143-144
  and Persian literature, 93
  and religious vigilantes, 86
  and Umayyads, 131
  union of church and state, 27
  and West, 141-142
Great Britain
  and colonialism, 138
  Islam in, 16, 150

INDEX

INDEX

CONTRIBUTORS

MASOUD KHEIRABADI is an Iranian American who immigrated to the United States in 1976. He lived for three years in Texas, where he received his M.S. in Agricultural Mechanization from Texas A&I University (later joined with Texas A&M). In 1979, he moved to Eugene, Oregon, and studied at the University of Oregon, where he received his M.A. and later Ph.D. in cultural geography. He has taught at the University of Oregon, Lewis & Clark College, and Marylhurst University. He currently teaches for the Humanities and International Studies Program at Portland State University.

Professor Kheirabadi's research interests deal with the Middle East and Islamic issues. He is particularly interested in the relationship between religion, politics, and development. He has published books and articles on these topics. Among his recent publications are *Iranian Cities: Formation and Development* and *Modern World Nations: Iran*.

ANN MARIE B. BAHR is Professor of Religious Studies at South Dakota State University. Her areas of teaching, research and writing include World Religions, New Testament, Religion in American Culture, and the Middle East. Her articles have appeared in *Annual Editions: World Religions 03/04* (Guilford, CT: McGraw-Hill, 2003), *The Journal of Ecumenical Studies*, and *Covenant for a New Creation: Ethics, Religion and Public Policy* (Maryknoll, NY: Orbis, 1991). Since 1999, she has authored a weekly newspaper column which analyzes the cultural significance of religious holidays. She has served as President of the Upper Midwest Region of the American Academy of Religion.

MARTIN E. MARTY, an ordained minister in the Evangelical Lutheran Church in America, is the Fairfax M. Cone Distinguished Service Professor Emeritus at the University of Chicago Divinity School, where he taught for thirty-five years. Marty has served as president of the American Academy of Religion, the American Society of Church History, and the American Catholic Historical Association, and was also a member of two U.S. presidential commissions. He is currently Senior Regent at St. Olaf College in Northfield, Minnesota. Marty has written more than fifty books, including the three-volume *Modern American Religion* (University of Chicago Press). His book *Righteous Empire* was a recipient of the National Book Award.